Restoring the Burnt Child

Restoring
the Burnt Child
A Primer

William Kloefkorn

University of Nebraska Press : Lincoln & London

Library of Congress Cataloging-in-
Publication Data
Kloefkorn, William.
Restoring the burnt child : a primer /
William Kloefkorn.
p. cm.
ISBN 0-8032-2759-0 (cl.: alk. paper) –
1. Kloefkorn, William – Childhood
and youth. 2. Kloefkorn, William –
Homes and haunts – Kansas.
3. Poets, American – 20th century –
Biography. 4. Kansas – Social life
and customs. 5. Kansas – Biography.
1. Title.
PS3561.L626Z476 2003 813'.54–dc21
2003042653

For my sister, Bernadine, and my brother, Johnny Lee

I bid you, mock not Eros:
He knows not doubt or shame.
And, unaware of proverbs,
The burnt child craves the flame.

CHRISTOPHER MORLEY

Restoring the Burnt Child

I

BELIEVE THIS MUCH: I had not intended to set our family home on fire.

I had instead intended to set my buddy R. D. Baker on fire, using as a flamethrower a large match from a box of Diamond matches taken from the kitchen. R. D. – Roland Duane – had likewise removed a box of matches from his own kitchen with the intention of beating me to the immolating punch.

It was nothing more than good, clean fun, this game we called firefly. It required speed and concentration and purpose – and the God-given ability to strike a match at full throttle and drop it burning down the shirt of the fleeing victim.

The truth is this: At the age of nine we didn't have much to do for entertainment in our little town in south central Kansas. There was the picture show, of course, the Rialto, but I couldn't afford the price of a ticket, and R. D., though he often carried some loose change in a front pocket of his blue overalls, was repeatedly warned by his parents that if he so much as darkened the door of the Rialto he would be whipped within an inch of his life. R. D.'s parents were Pentecostals who stoutly believed that moving pictures were of the devil – moving pictures and dances and earrings and lipstick and liquor and profanity and disobedience and backtalk and other human foibles and errancies too numerous to list. Their strict rules, of course, gave my buddy the daily challenge to defy them. He was a feisty young man with a mind of his own.

Soon enough we would be eleven; the Second World War would grow hotter and heavier, the Allies having landed on many beaches, among them the bloodiest, Omaha, and most of our friends would have well-supplied arsenals from which to draw the ordnance necessary to the conducting of brush-fire skirmishes on the home front.

Neither R. D. nor I owned a BB gun, but we had friends who did. So on a hot Saturday afternoon in early August, one year before the *Enola Gay* would drop an atomic bomb on Hiroshima, we borrowed a brace of Red Ryder BB guns from connections who in the interest of national security must remain anonymous.

But the acquiring of ammunition was not so easy; BBs, because of the war, were at a premium. We scavenged the neighborhood from one end to the other, at last locating a sleeve of those precious golden pellets in Gladden Woods's attic, where Gladden showed us several pinups he kept hidden from the two old-maid aunts he lived with.

Weapons and ammo in hand, we repaired to R. D.'s backyard, where a stack of old bricks provided a fort for him and the backside of a large elm's trunk provided protection for me. We divided the pellets, loaded our rifles, assumed our positions behind our fortifications, and opened fire.

I do not believe that either of us gave any thought whatsoever to the likelihood of someone being injured; the BB that brings down the bird surely is not sufficient unto bringing down the boy. At age eleven, the boy is immortal.

To conserve ammunition we aimed carefully and fired infrequently. I remember that certain aspects of the confrontation confused and disappointed me. For example, I found myself enormously attracted to the large trunk of the elm tree; I had no desire to attempt to expose myself to a flanking movement such as I saw in some of the movies that now I could afford to watch, thanks to an income from the mowing of several lawns.

And I was disappointed that the BBs did not richochet – or, if they did, the ricocheting did not produce the splendid whistling I heard from the near misses at the movies. I could follow the trajectory of the golden pellet, a trajectory at times so far off the mark that I wondered about the efficacy of my borrowed gun. But there was no whistling.

Now *richochet* is such a wonderful word that it is difficult not to admire it – the way it sits on the page, the sound it makes, whether spoken or unspoken. *Rich-o-chet*. So, too, *trajectory*. Look at it. Say it: *tra-jec-to-ry*. The awful war, for all its awfulness, brought me language I loved in spite of its deadly overtones. *Stu-ka*. *Mess-er-schmitt*. *Flak*.

During a succession of lulls R. D. had rearranged his wall of bricks to provide an opening through which he pointed his BB gun straight at the V behind which I, on my knees, pointed my own BB gun straight at him. I couldn't actually see much of his face; the aperture – *a-per-ture* – was small, and the barrel of the gun occupied most of its space.

Nonetheless – call it fate, chance, luck, divine intervention – I nailed him with a BB almost in the eye. Immediately he did the honorable thing – he stood with his hands raised, acknowledging defeat.

The BB was lodged in his forehead just above his right eyebrow. With a thumb and an index finger R. D. removed the pellet, holding it then in the palm of his hand as if cradling a badge of incredible courage. And I found myself envying that tiny golden badge, envying the one who held it, envying the humility it must have taken to admit defeat. I had won the battle, but somehow – and I knew this instinctively if not rationally – I had lost the war.

R. D. not only held the bullet whose impact he had managed to survive, but just as significantly he carried on his forehead the wound that would make him notorious on the playground and in the classroom – and at home, where, he would tell me the next day, he had told his father the truth and where, in turn, his father had whipped him.

And not with a belt, R. D. said, but with a strop. A razor strop. R. D. grinned when he said it: *strop*. Razor strop. It looks like a wide leather belt, R. D. said. My dad, he said, uses it to sharpen his razor.

I had not heard that word before. When R. D. said it, *strop*, it sounded like a wide leather belt making contact with bare flesh. Because, R. D. said, his father had told him to drop his britches and bend over, whereupon his father with Pentecostal fury applied the strop to R. D.'s bare flesh. Strop after strop, said Roland Duane.

Until, he reckoned, his daddy's arm became tired and he stopped. And would I like to see the red welts the strop left on R. D.'s butt?

I said no. I said it must have hurt.

R. D. grinned. He had perfect teeth. He was good looking – almost too much so – with dimples and thick dark hair and brown eyes and, now, a small insignia of distinction the size of a BB just above his right eyebrow.

Like a bastard, he said. Hurt like a bastard with its tail on fire.

I tried to imagine a bastard with its tail on fire. But I couldn't do it. I didn't know what a bastard was, beyond recognizing the word, so of course I had nothing of substance to affix a tail to.

R. D., by his own account, had suffered through the ordeal without crying or asking for mercy, perhaps because he knew that neither would move his father to reduce either the severity or the duration of the punishment. And, too, R. D. had kept the fateful BB and had squeezed it in his left palm, he said, throughout the stropping. He had since hidden the golden pellet, he said, in a place where not even God Himself could find it.

But the conflict with BB guns, the golden BB that almost found its way into R. D.'s eye, and the subsequent stropping lay in the future, crouching like something large but not definable; at the moment, I and my buddy were looking forward to setting someone on fire.

We met in the middle of the gravel road that separated our houses, each of us with a box of wooden matches, each intending to throw or drop the lighted match that would ignite the other. And I confess that my nervousness bordered on fear because I was very much aware of my opponent's agility and tenacity. I outweighed R. D. by more than a few pounds, but I could not begin to match his quickness, and I knew also that R. D. always, always intended to finish whatever it was he, or anyone else, started.

So there we were in the middle of the gravel road, early August, late afternoon, each holding a box of Diamond matches in a left hand, each with a right hand ready to dip into the half-open box to bring forth a match, strike it, and deliver it onto the body of the enemy. When one of us shouted, Go! the game of firefly would begin.

One of us shouted, Go!

R. D. turned quickly and headed for an open chunk of acreage just south of his stuccoed, one-story house. I ran after him, steadily losing ground until, at the center of the open field, R. D. stopped and waited. I slowed my pace. I knew what R. D. was up to; we had played this game before.

I slowed to a walk. When I was only about three paces away, I struck a match and tossed it at the bib of R. D.'s blue overalls. R. D. returned the favor. Both his match and mine fizzled. Each struck and delivered a second match. Again, each match fizzled.

Then with a catlike movement R. D. stood in front of me, cheek by jowl, his right hand striking matches with an energy akin to Pentecostal. With a movement I like to believe was also feline, I wheeled and fled. I circled the open field, R. D. on my heels; I could hear the striking of matches against the sandpaper side of the Diamond matchbox, but thus far I felt certain that none had ignited my shirt, which was blue and faded and short sleeved and had snaked its way down to me by way of an older cousin.

Oh, how I envied R. D.'s quickness, his explosive speed! He was lean and agile and never ran short of breath. My principal recourse, then, was the frequent deployment of the zigzag; R. D. might outrun me, might be at my very heels, but for all his swiftness he was not clairvoyant – he could not tell when, or how often, I might zig and zag, and it was this tactic that kept me in the game.

This tactic, and my decision to do something in violation of the rules: run into and through the house. Which I did, slamming the screen door behind me. Soon enough I heard the screen door slam again; R. D. was in hot pursuit.

I don't know why I thought of stopping suddenly in the kitchen, of turning just as suddenly to throw a sequence of lighted matches in the direction of R. D.'s surprised, good-looking face. But I did.

The matches failed to ignite my buddy, but at least one of them found the woodbox beside the range and ignited some papers that in turn ignited some wood that in turn ignited the kitchen that in turn . . .

Across the alley Archie Black was the first to see the smoke, then the flames. And it was Archie who called in the alarm.

I was far from the smoldering kitchen, lighting another match, when I heard the siren and saw the fire truck come to a heavy halt in our driveway. R. D., too, had heard the siren; I heard him say something sharp and unbecoming under his breath.

In unison, without speaking, we closed our matchboxes and left them one atop the other in a cluster of sunflowers. We approached the driveway to observe more clearly the proceedings.

If you have never watched a gaggle of small-town firefighters in action, you do not appreciate absolutely the meaning of mayhem. Our local firefighters were volunteers who, when the whistle at the power plant sounded, dropped whatever they had in their hands or on their minds and ran or drove in pretty much a straight line to the fire truck, whose long red body rested in a red-brick appendage to the power plant. The first to arrive would start the engine, perhaps, while the second to arrive would open the tall, white door. After two or three others had hopped onto the truck's running boards, the driver would put the truck in gear and roar through the open door with an almost divine unconcern for the lives of those on board or of those who, along the way, jumped on board – or of those who simply happened to be crossing the street on foot or in a vehicle. It is astonishing that, to my knowledge, our firefighters on their fire truck never sent to perdition a single innocent motorist or pedestrian.

It is equally astonishing that, having arrived at the scene of the conflagration, the firefighters sometimes managed to turn apparent mayhem into eventual order. I stood beside my buddy R. D. watching without yet appreciating this transformation.

Late afternoon. Early evening. We call it dusk. It's that time filled with light and no light, with men scrambling, with water enough to quench God's thirst pouring from the end of an almighty hose, with red in the form of a fire truck outglowing the sunset, with R. D. standing beside me, our eyes no doubt equivalent to saucers. R. D.'s whispered swearing was, as I perceived it, a form of respect, of reverence, perhaps of prayer.

Swearing can be like that, can't it – at times demeaning and ugly, at other times harmless if not in fact respectful. Chaucer in one of his stories makes a compelling distinction between the curse that comes from the heart and the one that doesn't, the former intended genuinely to disparage, the latter intended to amount only to an ineffectual blowing of smoke. His friar tells the story: A summoner, on his way to visit an innocent old woman he hopes to take monetary advantage of (pay me, woman – if not money, then at least a pot or a pan – and I'll see to it that your sins are forgiven), meets with a bad egg who turns out to be the devil himself. On their way they come across a farmer whose cart with its load of hay is stuck in the mud. The farmer, frustrated, curses his horses. "The devil with you . . . ," he says, "skin and bones!"

But the devil, so handy standing nearby, does not take the horses off to hell; instead, he watches as the horses continue to struggle, until finally they free the cart from the mire, whereupon the farmer praises them. So why didn't the devil deliver the horses to perdition? Because, he tells the summoner, their master's curse did not derive from the heart.

Later, when the summoner confronts the woman and attempts his extortion, he learns quickly enough that she is no pushover. She sees him for the bloodsucker he is and refuses to give him anything, not even a pot or a pan. Instead, she resorts to the curse:

I give the devil, with his rough, black hue,
Your body, and with it he can have my pan!

This time, because the curse comes from the innocent old woman's heart, the curse is honored. "You'll be in hell tonight," the fiend says to the summoner,

Where you can study our secrets to infinity
And learn more than a master of divinity.

9

R. D.'s whisperings, as he stood beside me, were an impressive mixture of curse and invective, some of the language, in fact, amounting to self-incriminations that I'm sure did not come from the heart – Well, I'll be damned, for example, and, Well, I'll be a son of a bitch!

We watched as mayhem somehow worked its own inscrutable magic, men and hose and water doing battle with flames that leapt and crackled and hissed as they consumed the kitchen walls, the kitchen table and chairs, the kitchen cupboards wherein lay the silverware that later, with a rag dipped in hot soapy water, I'd help my mother rub back to a reasonable brightness. Later, too, my mother would punish me in a manner both awkward and embarrassing: She would ask me to lie belly-down on her lap while she'd spank me, she doing most of the crying, my own crying chiefly a reaction to my mother's undeniable sorrow. Because, after all, she'd not really wanted to spank me – I was too large for such a punishment, and my mother was not much given to such a physical tactic. But I had done something inexcusable, meaning that I could not be excused – not without some form of unusual punishment. And certainly that punishment would have to be delivered by my mother; my father could not, would not, strike his son – never had and, goddammit, never would. Instead, he would clench his teeth and swear intensely through them, would do the clenching and the swearing with a conviction that impressed me more deeply than did any spanking I ever received from my mother.

I have thought a lot about my father's manner of swearing, thought about it many years ago when he was in his prime and have thought a lot about it off and on ever since. Mouth closed, teeth joined firmly, he would utter expletives for as long as the situation demanded, and it was my father himself who decided how long the situation demanded. When he saw the destroyed kitchen, for example, he did the clenching and the swearing for only a few seconds. He stood in the gravel driveway holding his black lunch bucket in his right hand, seeing, certainly, but at first not quite believing. When reality at last struck home, and with it its awesome magnitude, he did the clenching and the swearing. It was as if he somehow knew a disaster might occur but hadn't imagined that it would come in the form of a burned-out kitchen. So the teeth went clenched and the invectives erupted, guttural and garbled and expressive almost beyond belief.

At other times the clenching and the swearing would continue, with irregular intermissions, until the disaster had been corrected or redeemed. It was my father's way of sometimes getting something done.

The axle broke, of course, when the family vehicle was fully loaded with family and an assortment of Christmas gifts. We were beginning a trip to visit my paternal grandfather, who lived on a rock-infested quarter section in southeast Kansas. We had looked forward to the journey for many weeks; we didn't often venture beyond the city limits of my little hometown, so when the decision was made to travel one hundred and twenty miles to Grandfather's farm near Cedar Vale, each of us – my older sister, my younger brother, my mother, and my father – began to live lives of quiet exhilaration. When the moment for departure finally arrived, the black Ford serviced and loaded, we sat in our assigned places indulging an anticipatory silence worthy of church.

We were not yet out of the driveway, moving backward, when a sudden whump, concurrent with a sudden lowering of the rear portion of the vehicle, broke the silence. Father looked at Mother, who looked at him. Then slowly he opened his door to begin his ritual.

It was a ritual he performed whenever something went wrong with the family car, regardless of what might be its ailment. Step One: Circle the vehicle slowly, moving counterclockwise, stopping at each tire to kick it while saying the following: God-damn-you-dirty-son-of-a-bitching-bastard-all-to-hell, anyway. Utter the sentence with the teeth clenched, and utter it as if uttering it for the first time, as if its profound intensity were somewhat, if not in fact chiefly, the result of on-the-spot improvisation.

Step Two: Raise the hood, regardless of whether the breakdown has anything at all to do with the engine. Examine the engine as, at irregular intervals, you utter additional expletives. Reach a hand to touch this or that – a plug, a coil wire, a doohickey – until you have either scorched or soiled the hand, then step back and shake the head slowly.

Step Three: Move to the trunk, open it, and begin a search for the toolbox. When the box is located, remove it from the trunk and sift through its contents. Leave some of the instruments in the box, the others lying in an assortment of attitudes on the ground. At irregular intervals utter whatever invectives inspiration demands.

Repeat this triad of steps until help arrives.

As it did on that Saturday morning when the axle broke. From somewhere, perhaps nowhere, several men materialized, one of them knowledgeable about broken axles, another willing to drive to Timbuktu to barter for a new one, several others to remain behind to remove the broken axle and make everything ready for its replacement.

The performing of a miracle is a curious thing, even under the most favorable circumstances. But even more curious than the performing is the standing aside to watch as it is being performed. I did this. I stood far to one side, watching, waiting, taking it in, every atom of it, as each worker performed his part. The old axle was removed. Soon enough a new axle, behold, appeared and was put into place. Nouns that I had paid little attention to before now became certifiable nuggets on the bottom of the prospector's pan. *Lug nut. Crescent. Gasket. Grease.*

My obligation in this unfolding of a miracle was to do whatever was necessary to keep my overalls clean. So I stood off to one side and witnessed the resurrection of a vehicle. And, behold, when the workers said to the deceased, Come forth! the deceased came forth – she started, she hummed, and when my father shifted her into reverse, she moved backward. Selah.

When R. D. suggested that we move closer to the fire, I agreed, and we walked toward the flames. They were well under control now, which perhaps accounts for our courage – until their heat compelled us to stop. The flames, to my surprise, were unbelievably hot, so hot that even today I measure hotness by the hotness of our burning kitchen. So how hot might hell be? Well, hotter than our burning kitchen. Jesus. Can you imagine?

That day the axle broke we drove to my grandfather's farm without any further need to resort to miracles, though a flurry of snow just south of Danville turned my father's impish grin to a frown. It worried me, too, but I reckoned that if I concentrated hard enough my concentration would help us survive the flurry. At my right my older sister sat looking out the window, serene, confident, dutiful, her yellow curls, if they hadn't belonged to my older sister, beautiful. At my left my little brother sat slumped against the door, snoring like a little moron. Which meant that I alone must do the concentrating. If the snow should become heavier and the road slick, my father, whose driving was not infallible, would need all the help he could get.

Faith. Faith is what happens when you cannot concentrate any longer, when willpower turns to slush, when finally you close your eyes and believe, as you drift into nihility, that when you awaken you will be there.

2

. . . heat so near
so everywhere
it sucked the body empty.
And they tell me
it was a neighbor
from across the alley
who made the call,
and when I looked at the spot
where the match had been,
and the kitchen,
and into the eyes of the woman
who whipped me raw,
then rocked me,
I said Yes Yes Yes
to the birth of fire.

THE NEIGHBOR WAS Archie Black, and I believe the spot where I had thrown the match – or several matches, because I know that, in a frenzy, I tossed more than one – was somewhere in the vicinity of the woodbox beside the range, a cardboard box that held not only wood and cobs but also some remnants of newspapers. And to be honest I must confess that my mother did not whip me raw; she spanked me, yes, and she cried as she spanked, and when she had cried herself out she moved her large legs back and forth to simulate, I'm guessing, a type of rocking. Thus did she punish her oversized nine-year-old son, and thus did fire, for me, become truly born.

I had heard of fire before, certainly, and I had seen it, most consistently in the bellies of the kitchen range and the Warm Morning woodstove in the living room. But these fires, for all their heat, were contained, stoked and manipulated and left to die out when the meal was ready or it came time to go to bed. The fire that destroyed our kitchen, however, fought mightily against containment; it raged and flared and threatened to consume the entire house.

I knew fire also by way of a relentless procession of preachers who used the word as the first syllable of a four-syllable word – *fireandbrimstone*. I remember one of these dervishes in particular – a thick, wide woman who called herself Sister Hook. She had a round, chubby face and a large mouth that, open, revealed two rows of snow-white teeth and a red tongue that had I known the word at the time I might have identified as a strop. She wore her blonde hair in a large bun secured with small, multicolored combs. Her shoes were black and ankle-high, her dresses, perhaps in their earlier incarnations, flowered bedsheets.

Sister Hook conducted a weeklong tent revival one summer, her tent pitched at the center of a catalpa grove three miles west of town. Sand Creek defined the eastern edge of the grove, wheat stubble to the north and west, and a thin macadam highway two hundred yards to the south. In early August, when the meetings began, the catalpas were in full bloom, their beans hanging long and plentiful among the leaves.

I attended the meetings because my grandfather invited me – picked me up in his old Chevrolet and after the service, which sometimes lasted halfway into eternity, delivered me home. Grandfather and Grandmother, in spite of their inveterate belief in a just and merciful God, were less than one year away from losing their farm, a tidy, productive quarter section four miles north of town. A mix-up at the grain elevator would somehow be the first domino to fall; thereafter, an inscrutable series of additional falling dominoes would result in my grandparents' losing the farm and moving to a much less fertile acreage in southeastern Kansas near Cedar Vale.

The mix-up would probably not be my grandfather's fault. On the other hand, the mix-up, having occurred, probably, or maybe, would be augmented by my grandfather's constitutional inability to compromise. He was a large, jovial German who, when challenged, laid his joviality off to one side and in its place substituted a stubbornness more than equal to that of a Missouri mule. So he lost the farm.

But not quite yet. At the moment, he is driving me to a revival meeting; we are in his old off-green four-door Chevrolet moving west on a narrow macadam highway toward a large grove of catalpas at the center of which I will see, for the first time, Sister Hook's mammoth tent, its sides rolled up, its top like a circus tent held aloft with poles the size of pillars to which are tied hemp ropes thick as bullsnakes, their ends knotted to wooden stakes that must surely have been driven into the ground all the way to China. We are driving without Grandmother, who this evening, and tomorrow evening and the next, is and will be at the farmhouse alone, doing whatever a petite human dynamo does when the homestead is free of males.

And this is a quaint circumstance. I thought so at the time, though I was only eight, and I think so today, though I am somewhat older. Because Grandmother, you see, was far more evangelical – if that's the correct word – than was Grandfather. She was the one who gave her grandchildren, over and over, the same gift: a brightly painted pencil inscribed with a verse from the Bible. Sometimes the verse was so extensive that the tiny font was difficult to decipher: *John 3:16 For God so loved the world. . . .* I collected these pencils, wrote with them, sharpened them with an old Barlow, and read them until their messages, behold, had become sawdust.

Always it was Grandmother who in her own half-cheerful way did the proselytizing, and it was Grandmother who, with a vengeance, disapproved of most forms of entertainment.

Consider, for example, the night of the leaky accordion: Grandfather's ancient black-and-red accordion had a pinhole in its bellows, so of course it leaked air – not a lot of air but enough to influence the quality of the tone that emerged from the accordion's mystical chambers. Attach this somewhat off tone to my grandfather's sandpaper baritone and you have, as far as this grandchild was concerned, a union made in heaven.

Grandmother, though, apparently thought otherwise. So when Grandfather brought out the accordion – which was painfully infrequent – and cozied himself in his favorite rocker and prepared himself to sing a hymn or two, Grandmother would excuse herself and trot into the nearby kitchen, where throughout the concert she would busy herself with her pots and pans, putting together ingredients for a cake, perhaps, or a pie, the tablespoon as it scraped the sides of the mixing bowl making sounds that maybe Grandmother wanted us to be aware of.

The concert, in any case, would proceed, Grandfather in his wide rocker slightly rocking as he sang, say, "Blessed Assurance," I and my sister and brother sitting cross-legged on the pine floor, loving each and every element of the moment, even those that we didn't understand. Grandfather, working the leaky bellows, rocking his large, jovial German body to keep the rocker rocking, would lean back his head and close his eyes and sing as if his life depended upon the singing, as no doubt he believed it did: *This is my story, this is my song, praising my savior all the day long. . . .*

I now believe that Grandmother viewed Grandfather's singing and playing as an example of theater gone too far – or, if not excessive theatricality in and of itself, as a prelude to undue entertainment. Because if Grandfather played the accordion and performed several hymns, we could be certain that, at the conclusion of any given hymn, he would recite a story that he had memorized when in his youth he had belonged to what he called a "literary." These were comic pieces whose heroes included a farmer who had difficulty retrieving eggs from beneath a possessive hen, and to Noah, who had his own difficulties as he saw to the loading of the ark.

It was the story of Noah and the ark that one late evening caused Grandmother to rattle the pots and pans more liberally than ever before, no doubt because the story involved a biblical figure who called into question the rationality of God's judgment. Is it really necessary to build such a ship? Why take along only two of each living animal – two sheep, two goats, two horses? (Grandfather would have left the sheep and goats behind and, in their places, would have taken additional horses, preferring horses to all other beasts of burden, including John Deere tractors.) And, too, the story, as Grandfather recited it, was amusing, its refrain – *and there was Ham and there was Shem and there was Japheth, ah, and they all ran into the ark, ah* – making no sense whatsoever, but its lyricism providing an undeniable aural delight. My older sister would giggle, and so would I, and my little brother, Johnny, not to be outdone, would giggle, too.

We were a small congregation of listeners and gigglers, with Grandfather as both preacher and entertainer, a combination that Grandmother could not abide. But we listened and giggled anyway, and the rattling of the pots and pans increased as our heretical joy increased until, behold, Grandfather stopped his story in midsentence and, rising slowly from the rocker, walked then slowly to the kitchen. I turned my head to see that my sister's head, too, was turned, and I watched and listened very carefully. The rattling of the pots and pans stopped. I could hear a dialogue of whispering, but I could not discern what was being said. The moment, for reasons I could not put my child's finger on, had the feeling and the texture of a funeral, though I didn't then know much about funerals, having attended only the service conducted for a classmate who had died from something I could not pronounce. What had suddenly fallen inside the farmhouse was a *hush*, and though I didn't know the word I knew the sensation. A palpable hush had fallen, and the whispering only made it all the more palpable.

When Grandfather returned to the rocker he was smiling. He sat down and with his right hand lifted the accordion from the floor. But he did not play, not yet. He held the old red-and-black instrument in his lap as if cradling a child while he finished his account of Noah and the ark. *And there was Ham and there was Shem and there was Japheth, ah, and they all ran into the ark, ah*. Then he raised the accordion and began to sing. He was a dirt farmer who most of his waking hours farmed dirt. He harnessed horses and milked cows and fed chickens and, using an iron slip the size of a small building, dug a pond to catch occasional rainwater cascading down a rocky hill. But now he was, amazingly, someone else – a large man in blue overalls and a blue workshirt playing, of all things, a leaky accordion while singing, of all things, "Blessed Assurance." And his wife, my grandmother, was in the kitchen mixing ingredients for a cake or a pie, something sweet deriving from her grand disapproval. *This is my story, this is my song.* . . .

The sun was about to set when we arrived at the revival site. The tent was in place at the center of the catalpa grove, and people were standing in clusters or sitting on brown metal folding chairs. The chairs formed two long sections with a wide aisle between them. Woodchips and sawdust provided a thick mat for the chairs to rest on, and at the front of the tent a substantial platform of two-by-tens provided a solid foundation for a pulpit and several folding chairs that later I'd learn were there to accommodate a band – two trumpets, one clarinet, one trombone, one flute, one bass horn, one snare drum, and a piano.

Small tents of varied shapes and colors stood among the catalpas; these belonged to those hardy souls who intended to make a full week of it, full week meaning today, Monday, through very late next Sunday night. Small ropes had been strung from one tree to another to provide lines for the hanging out of clothes, and already an assortment of clothes had been hung out. The place appeared to be a small village sprung up overnight, as in fact it pretty much was. Or perhaps, to be more precise, the place looked like it had been taken over by a prolific family, assorted children as well as adults moving into and out of the tents.

Grandfather parked the car in a cleared-off expanse at the western edge of the grove and told me not to wander too far away. Wander too far away? I had no intention of wandering anywhere. I would stay beside my grandfather come hell or high water.

As it turned out both hell and high water came, but not on that first night. They would occur on Sunday night when the revival reached its highest, and thus hottest, peak.

Grandfather did not go directly to the big tent at the center of the grove. Instead, he went to several of the smaller tents where he talked briefly with folks he knew – a neighbor, maybe, or a man who wasn't a neighbor but who regularly attended services at the Assembly of God church. The sun, meanwhile, was about to set, and when it did an amazing network of lights suddenly went on, lights that had been strung around the top and inside of the big tent and lines of bulbs hanging from the branches of the catalpas.

Grandfather seemed to be feeling unusually good. He laughed with the people he talked with; he appeared almost comfortable in clothes that I thought strange, if not downright inappropriate: black dress shoes, a tan suit barely wrinkled, white shirt and a red tie with a small knot, and, in his left hand, a black, dog-eared Bible.

Sister Hook carried a black, dog-eared Bible, too, but hers was easily twice the size of Grandfather's; throughout the service she would hold the book first in one hand, then in the other, at times slapping it with her free hand, at other times slapping it against the top of the pulpit: *slap* and *slap* and *slap*, until I'd fully expected the pulpit to say something in its own defense, or to break down and ask for mercy.

By the time Grandfather and I had reached the big top it was half filled; tenters had been joined by people from my town, many of whom I recognized, as well as strangers from neighboring towns – Sharon, Medicine Lodge, Kiowa, Hazelton, and probably others from towns farther away. Grandfather had been visiting with a man who stood in front of his small blue tent when I heard the band begin the service – *Shall we gather at the river?* Yes, we shall, though the river isn't much to speak of, a thin serpentining of sand along the eastern edge of the grove, sand that occasionally felt the rush of water, as it had earlier today, a shower that came straight down from Sister Hook's heaven, rainwater that made this Monday night at the revival meeting smell like – what?

Like the cave my brother and I dug in our backyard, or in one of them, our family having moved from one house to another in unsuccessful attempts to better itself. We dug the cave slowly, very slowly, thanks to a dull shovel and soil that under a layer of buffalo grass was at least as firm as a fanatic's conviction. But we persisted: One leg over the other the dog walks to Dover. When at last we had a hole deep enough to suggest that, if we lived long enough, we might succeed, we took to hauling the dirt up and out with the aid of a discarded milk bucket: Standing in the hole, I would pester the stubborn dirt with the dull shovel until I had filled the bucket, whereupon my little brother, standing topside and holding fast to the rope, whose trailing end was tied to the handle of the bucket, would hoist the bucket and, on those occasions when he didn't lose his grip, dump its contents on the buffalo grass behind him.

It was pretty much a flawless system, we believed, though our mother, born to worry, saw it as the probable means to a fatal end. The sides will cave in, she said, or, what is worse, the top will collapse and you will be smothered to death, as sure as sin. *As sure as sin*. This expression had been my introduction to the inevitability of badness. *As sure as sin*. Sin, then, was a certainty and so, too, the demise of Billy and his little brother, Johnny, if they persisted in digging that infernal cave.

We persisted. Mother objected, of course, but not to the point of any threat. And so it came to pass that the hole, bucket by bucket, deepened, and the pile of Kansas dirt behind my brother grew higher and higher. Unfortunately, he had not started the pile far enough behind him so that by the time the hole was sufficiently deep, dirt from the pile began to slide down into the hole. We took turns with the shovel then, removing the dirt from here to create a new pile over there.

By the middle of July, or perhaps August, we had finished not only digging the hole and trimming its sides – it measured two strides in one direction and three point five strides in the other – but we also had dug a tunnel that led into the finished hole. Now we had only to provide a roof of scrap lumber, cardboard, and gunnysacks, these three, and dirt from the relocated pile of dirt to cover them. Under the dirt, the lath and the cardboard and the gunnysacks sagged a little, but probably they would not collapse and smother us to death. We provided a roof for the tunnel also, leaving a small hole at its end to serve as the entrance. The cave, our hide-out, was finished.

But the point here is not that we finished digging and covering the cave or that Mother foretold our early, suffocating deaths; the point is that there is no smell quite like the smell of a hand-dug cave, especially when you enter the cave shortly after a rainfall.

We did this, my brother and I, after a brief shower, I holding an old Barlow in my right hand, Johnny holding a small candle, each of us with half a dozen kitchen matches in our pockets. You see, we had anticipated the need for light because we had spent some earlier time in the cave without light and the darkness had been less excit-ing than we had anticipated. So on this occasion we entered the tunnel with the wherewithal to disperse the darkness.

With my pocket knife I went to work cutting a small recess into the south wall; then I carved a hole into the floor of the recess to accommodate the candle. I placed one end of the candle into the hole, and my little brother, so smoothly you might confuse him with a professional, struck a match against the latch on the bib of his overalls and, behold, there was light.

True, the flame on the candle flickered, there being a minor shortage of oxygen, but the flickering served to enhance more than disturb our universe. In the eerie movements of light everything seemed different if not reborn, and the effluvium from dark, damp earth entered the nose like an olfactory blessing. And my little brother, barefoot and shirtless inside his overalls, could not stop grinning. He had been a cog on a gear that had turned and turned until it accomplished a mission of immense importance, and now he was enjoying the fruits of that gear's labor, the spoils that derive from persistence.

> Into a small puddle made possible by a small leak in the roof
> my brother works his toes. By the time the candle
> has spent itself, my brother's feet,
> up to the ankles, up almost
> to the high cuffs on his overalls,
> are lost in ooze.

Lost in ooze also were our thoughts, thoughts enhanced by what we sensed as we inhaled, though the word for it would not arrive until many years later. *Fe-cun-di-ty*. We sat in the midst of impending plenty, ripeness, now that the candle had spent itself, made manifest in the nose. And I thought that if I could see, I might see fingers scraping clay, inventing claws. Is this actually what I thought? Perhaps. Fecundity. Is this actually what I sensed? Perhaps. In any case, the olfactory pleasure could not be denied. *Fecundity*, the word, be damned. I inhaled deeply, again and again, not knowing what now I believe I know: the existence of gravity before the advent of Newton's law.

The afternoon shower had fallen not only on rope and canvas, bunchgrass and catalpa, but also on the woodchips and the sawdust around the edges of the big tent, and when I inhaled I could smell again the sides of the cave and its roof with a crisscrossing of laths and slats, cardboard and gunnysacks, and the soil that, rained on, caused the roof to sag, perhaps uncomfortably. Grandfather and I sat near the center of the southern section, Grandfather's back straight as an arrow, his dog-eared Bible held easily in place on his right leg.

After "Shall We Gather at the River," the band played "Power in the Blood" until Sister Hook, pacing the platform, smiling a large smile, smacking her free hand against her Bible, could contain herself no longer, at which point she erupted into song, and of course the congregation soon sang along with her. *There is power, power, power, power, wonder-working power, in the blood of the Lamb. . . .*

Such remarkable singing! And not just the singing but the sounds that came forth from the instruments, each at irregular intervals taking its turn in the spotlight. I especially enjoyed the snare drum because I had dreams of one day being a consummate percussionist; but each instrument, not alone the drum, spoke its part with a gusto that, joined with the voices of Sister Hook and the congregation, constituted roll after roll of thunder.

I could no longer smell the earthy sides of the cave, nor did I care to. An aural bombardment had forced the nose to yield to the ear – and to the eye, because the movements of Sister Hook, and the piano player, a large, elderly woman who bounced like a youngster on the piano bench, were so filled with what my father surely would have called piss and vinegar that the eye could not avoid their magnificence.

That first service is both a rumble and a blur; it had a beginning, yes, with the playing and the singing, and a middle, too, with its testimonials and freewill offering and sermon that focused sharply and deadly on the subjects of power and blood, Sister Hook on several occasions illustrating her points with husky solos (*Are you washed in the blood, in the soul-cleansing blood of the Lamb? Are your garments spotless, are they white as snow, are you washed in the blood of the Lamb?*). Then, to my further amazement, Sister Hook retreated to the rear of the platform and brought forth something large and upright that turned out to be a rolled-up scroll on which the evangelist herself had painted not only the entire history of humankind but also its future. I did not know at the time the extent of the scroll, and would not know until the final service on Sunday night. Tonight I would feast exclusively at the table of portent, meaning that Sister Hook would show us only several feet of her inclusive masterwork.

She began at the beginning, of course, with the creation of heaven and earth, both painted in spectacular colors by the hand of Sister Hook, both unrolled slowly by a young, skinny, lily-white man with heavily lubricated black hair. He watched Sister Hook intently as he did the unrolling; obviously he did not want to show the congregation more of the painting than the words of Sister Hook had revealed. It was a masterpiece of teamwork, I thought, and certainly the paintings of the heavens and the earth clearly established Sister Hook as a very gifted artist. Moon and stars and clouds, trees and rocks and hills and meadows, animals here and there, all of them looking contented, birds flying and in nests and sitting on branches, and an assortment of fields – though man had not yet been created to plant them – of corn and alfalfa and wheat. And again Sister

27

Hook burst into song: *Sowing in the morning, sowing seeds of kindness, sowing in the noon-tide and the dewy eve.* . . . With her stentorian voice Sister Hook brought in the sheaves, then more sheaves, then nodded to her accomplice, who methodically and precisely fed the scroll back into its holder.

Sister Hook told us then that each evening she would (1) review what she had covered the previous evening, and (2) reveal a further portion of the scroll until all of the past had been unrolled and all of the future, with documentation from the Scriptures, foretold.

It seemed to me that Sister Hook's forecast pretty much closed out the middle section of the service; the young man with the flour-white face had secured the scroll in its folder, had carried it then to the back of the platform, and had disappeared as uneventfully as he had earlier materialized.

There wasn't much of a segue into the third and final portion of the service. Sister Hook moved swiftly into more hymns, the band behind her squealing and tooting and thumping its support, the portly woman at the piano placing her body at risk as she bobbed and bounced atop the piano bench, old feline on a hot tin roof. Then more testimonials, all of them spontaneous, all of the speakers having apparently caught Sister Hook's fever, her cup flowing and then overflowing with that urine and vinegar. Many prayers, too, some of them finding their way into the testimonials, others deriving from worshipers who wanted to say something but didn't want to reveal anything unduly intimate.

Then, finally, a call to the altar, Sister Hook exhorting anyone who felt the Holy Spirit working in him to heed that call and walk down that aisle and kneel at this altar and confess his sins and be thereby saved and, if the Spirit persists, sanctified and set aside for the everlasting glory of Christ our Savior, amen.

After each exhortation the evangelist would sing a hymn, or part of a hymn – *Just as I am, without one plea, but that his blood was shed for me.* . . . *O lamb of God, I come, I come.* . . . Several in the congregation, young and old, stood and made their way down the aisle to the altar. Their moving ruffled the woodchips and the sawdust, and I could see the face of my little brother in the flickering candlelight, face grinning like a gopher, and I inhaled that moment – the face, the sides of the cave, the concept of fecundity.

I looked at Grandfather, whose back was as straight now as it had been a century or so ago when the service began. He turned his head and smiled. He did not go to the altar.

Before long, the altar – the front edge of the two-by-tens that served as a raised platform – was lined with kneeling penitents, their weeping and shouting and praying as if some divinely sanctioned form of mayhem. And more blood from the mouth of Sister Hook, and more lambs. *O lamb of God, I come, I come.* . . . Sister Hook with immense patience took her time as she moved from one kneeler to another, touching the tops of their heads with her free hand, closing her eyes and tilting back her head and praying, and of course bursting into occasional song: *Almost persuaded, now, to believe* . . .

This final part of the service ended as the participants, by degrees, became too exhausted to carry on. And though Grandfather and I did not stay until the last note sounded, the final word uttered, it was nonetheless quite late when we climbed into the waiting Chevrolet and headed home. I was sleepy, and the humming of the tires on the macadam highway very nearly lulled me to sleep. Grandfather didn't say anything until we reached the city limits. Lights along the sides of the street made my grandfather's face appear somehow very soft, very mellow. He looked at me and said, Son (though I wasn't his son; I was his grandson), what do you think?

It didn't take me long to figure out what it was that Mother told Grandfather the following evening when he picked me up: Could you maybe bring the boy home a little earlier?

I figured out some other things, too, as the evenings rolled along, or at least I believe I did. First, it occurred to me that Grandfather, though interested in what Sister Hook had to say, was perhaps almost equally interested in talking with some acquaintances before each service began. My grandfather was not really very gregarious; he was too busy with his handful of cattle and his hogs and chickens and team of horses to do a lot of socializing. His involvement with others outside the family was mostly a matter of ritual: to the Champlin station before prayer meeting on Wednesday evening, to Moulton's grocery store on Saturday night. Our early arrival at the campground, too, became a part of another ritual: park the Chevrolet, visit with several folks at their makeshift tents, find a place – always the same place, near the center of the southern section – settle onto folding metal chairs that were not all that easy to settle onto, then sit back and absorb the service.

Then, too, Grandfather was a member of a church – the Assembly of God – that was not altogether popular, at least if judged by its membership. His church was the smallest among the seven churches in Attica, a one-room, stuccoed structure that for Sunday school could be divided into several cubbyholes by pulling white cotton curtains along a network of wires. No other church in town could boast such modesty; no other church in town, in winter, could claim to be heated by a corpulent woodstove placed precisely in the center of an only room. Go to a morning service there in January and watch this stove with its isinglass windows scorch those nearest to it while providing only a promise to those farthest away.

Such a building did not attract many customers, and those that it did attract tended to be those who were (1) poor to the edge, or over the edge, of indigence, and (2) those who, maybe because of a lack of funds, were not very widely read. And, yes, it bothered me to admit that my grandparents were a trifle poor – as indeed my parents were also – and that their interest in reading much of anything beyond the Scriptures pretty much ended when they joined the Assemblies.

And maybe Grandfather, when he talked with some of his friends at their little tents, discussed not only the price of wheat and hogs but also the likelihood of their not being able to hang on, of their losing their farms to those big shots too nebulous ever to be confronted personally or nailed down from a distance. Maybe my grandfather had a premonition; maybe, as Sister Hook preached of a far-off Armageddon, my grandfather was sitting in his place on that metal chair worrying his head half off about tomorrow.

And maybe Grandmother wasn't with us because she wanted to leave all things political to Grandfather; maybe she felt that some ugly discussions might erupt and she wanted no part of such ugliness. Or maybe she believed that at camp meetings even her own church's theatrics went too far. Better, maybe, to do at least some of her praying in a closet, her kitchen, that sanctuary that neither a ranting Sister Hook nor a leaky bellows could corrupt. Just maybe.

And finally I figured out, this more than maybe, that the service I had watched and heard on Monday night was not the same as the one I sat witness to on Sunday. Because Monday night's performance, as it turned out, was only a warmup, only a dress rehearsal for the final production. There were overlappings and repetitions, of course, as there had been throughout the week, but the grand finale put them all to mortal shame.

My own personal interest in the festivities waxed as the festivities themselves did. Put simply, I was hooked on Sister Hook, on her rotundity no less than her energy and her husky voice, how words and music rolled from her cavernous mouth with such ease and continuity. As one service moved into another she seemed herself to be hooked on herself, as if her name were no more identification than description. But most especially I was hooked on her scroll; as the lean young man with the pasty face and the black, well-greased hair unfurled the scroll from its anchor end to hold it at the other end, making of himself a subaltern deity, like Hermes at the beck and call of his father, Zeus, I sat transfixed. By the end of the Saturday night service, all of the past, as edited by Sister Hook, had been covered with brilliant and often disturbing illustrations – Eve with her serpent in the Garden, Cain slaying his brother, Jericho, and Moses and Babel and Jonah and Pharaoh and a golden calf and a burning bush and Solomon and the jawbone of an ass and other folks and events too numerous either to catalog or explain or for me, then or now, to put into any semblance of an accurate chronology. My only interest in chronology was that of knowing, or of being told, which was the past and which the future. My interest lay chiefly in the paintings, in their bold and lurid colors, in the greenness of the green eyes of the villains, in the redness of the various shades of red that provided a fearful and gut-wrenching motif – red as in blood, certainly (*Are you washed in the blood, in the soul-cleansing blood of the Lamb?*), but also red as in fire, as in joining heat to sulfur, as in fireandbrimstone, as in heat unspeakable joined to time eternal.

I was a young boy trying to assimilate more than a young boy can, even a young boy with a quietly wise and surely immortal grandfather sitting upright beside him.

The service that Sunday night began almost on schedule. Our off-green Chevrolet had been parked in the makeshift lot at the western edge of the catalpa grove (I say *our* Chevrolet because by now it belonged to me as well as to Grandfather, I having sat in its front seat for several consecutive evenings inhaling the effluvia of its upholstery, effluvia of milk and manure and salty horsehair from the gargantuan bodies of Grandfather's team), and we had made our rounds of those small familiar tents, Grandfather speaking of crops and of rumors of crops, and had heard the call to worship from the band – again, as before, *Shall we gather at the river?* – and had found our seats near the center of the southern half section of chairs. Grandfather in his tan suit, now considerably wrinkled, sat regally in his chair, his dog-eared Bible at rest on his right leg, his light-headed grandson beside him, wonderfully lost in the curious hedgerows of expectancy.

Ex-pec-tan-cy. I expected – what? Well, more than I had experienced the night before, because the night before had been more intense than its own night before. I was aware that a buildup was taking place, and I couldn't wait to learn what it might finally lead to and end with.

3

SUCH MUSIC! More of it, and louder – the trombone sonorously flatulent, the drummer, having apparently caught the heebie-jeebies from the pianist, bouncing like a rubber ball on his stool as the trumpets and the clarinet joined the trombone's lovely baritone to guide him through "I Will Sing the Wondrous Story" and "Beulah Land" and "Leaning on the Everlasting Arms." Jesus. I found myself at times humming along, as were many others (the big tent was filled to overflowing), until the humming gave way to a murmuring of words, the murmuring to full-blown singing, the full-blown singing to occasional whoops, Sister Hook on the platform beside the pulpit with her fleshy arms orchestrating everything. When she motioned to the congregation to get to its feet, it did so, and when I stood on my chair to have a better view, Grandfather did not say no.

Already mayhem had begun to ride high in its saddle, and this was only the beginning. And in the beginning, Sister Hook said following prayers and testimonials and more prayers and two more hymns from the orchestra, God created the heavens and the earth. And the universe, she said, was without shape or form, so what do you suppose God did? He gave them shape and form, as He gave shape and form to first Adam, then Eve, and He saw that the shape and the form were good, and He said so, and if God says something is so then *it is so*.

Of course I cannot remember exactly what Sister Hook said, or the order, exactly, in which she said it. I can remember very clearly the many and varied expressions on her face, from deep sorrow, complete with tears, to ecstasy, her cheeks pink, her smile wide, her white teeth glinting, her tongue a redness honing every word. But her words swam downstream in a current much too swift ever to be slowed or diverted with anything less substantial than an all-out dam. Tonight, she said, we are standing on the promises of Christ our King, standing here in this grove of God's green trees, standing here where nothing but the blood of Jesus can wash us and make us whole. Praise Jesus! Praise his precious blood! We are, she said, standing on the promises that cannot fail, standing here in a place that is not our home – not this grove, not this state of Kansas, not this nation – for, she said, this world is not our home; we are simply passing through, our treasures being, she said, laid up elsewhere, elsewhere being, she said, Beulah Land, where we will stand on the eternal mountain under a cloudless sky, where standing there we will drink at that fountain that never shall run dry, shall feast, she said, on manna from a bountiful supply, for we shall be dwelling, she said, in Beulah Land.

She sang the song then, "Beulah Land," all four verses, the congregation insofar as it knew the words singing along with her, the band with perhaps more volume than necessary backing her up. The palm of Grandfather's right hand kept time against the black cover of his dog-eared Bible, and I saw on his face, at the side of his face, the nearer edge of a smile that suggested a combination of pleasure and amusement. I could never be certain, of course, of what my grandfather was thinking; one of several sons in a family of immigrants from southern Germany, he had escaped the tyranny of a father who had escaped the tyranny of a fatherland, and my own father, in turn, had escaped the confines, if not the tyranny, of a meager farm by marrying a German woman whose German parents disapproved of him. Jesus. When the roll is called up yonder, how many of us, do you suppose, will be there?

Sister Hook reminded us that Christ left His home in glory to assume the cross at Calvary. Oh what a friend, she said, we have in Jesus, who bears all of our sins, all of our griefs, and because He does this we will join Him in the sweet by and by, will join with Him, and with friends and loved ones and with all others who give their hearts to Him, at a land that, she said, is fairer than day. Oh we shall sing on that beautiful shore, she said, the me-lo-di-ous songs of the blessed, all of us then whiter than snow, our transgressions having been washed away by the blood that flowed from Immanuel's veins. Hallelujah! Oh we're marching to Zion, she said, to Zion, to Zion! Oh we're marching upward to Zion, Zion, she said – her eyes closed, her Bible open in her left hand – that beautiful city of God!

Earlier, riding in the Chevrolet on the macadam highway, Grandfather and I watched the sun disappear behind a bank of gray, billowing clouds. I looked at Grandfather looking at the clouds. He frowned. Might have some rain in them, he said. Maybe some wind.

Maybe some wind. Sister Hook was well into her explication of the future, of what all of us could expect if we didn't repent, when *some wind* struck, followed by *some lightning*, then *some thunder*, then *some rain* – enough rain, it seemed to me, to offer serious competition for Noah, *and there was Ham and there was Shem and there was Japheth, ah, and they all ran into the ark, ah* – the bellows of the giant tent leaking air until, behold, a small legion of men, appearing from nowhere, rolled down the sides of the tent and secured them with ropes and stakes, and the service, as if inexorably, rolled on.

Sister Hook scarcely missed a beat. The scroll was intact, thanks to our faithful flour-faced subaltern serving as ballast at the scroll's far end; he had held it down, his countenance totally free of both fear and irony, and he stood as tall almost as the scroll itself while Sister Hook, now using what appeared to be a length of dead catalpa as a pointer, preached on, her husky, Old Testament voice not one whit cowed by the thunder and the rain.

The artwork on the scroll had become so busy with images that it was difficult to determine where one disaster ended and another began. And principally it was the disaster, the fall, the human misfortune that seemed to compel Sister Hook – mayhem piled on mayhem without so much as a dram of balm, and with numbers serving as an incremental repetition: seven vials, seven dooms, seven kings. And there were many, many visions, too, and many bowls – of wrath, of fornication, of Babylon, of frogs and dragons, of Gog and Magog, of chariots and slaves and harlots and abominations, of fowls filled with the flesh of false prophets and their armies. And other litanies, most of which I could not connect – brass and iron, scarlet and silk, gold and silver, stones, ointments, flour, oil, frankincense, wine, beasts, wheat, sheep, cinnamon.

Rain pounded the tent top, and the sides of the tent flapped and groaned but did not break free of their moorings. Thunder broke suddenly and violently and unpredictably, as if Sister Hook's vociferous homily were in need of divine punctuation. Each flash of lightning gave the tent's canvas a momentary glow that in a context of grisly doom seemed somehow appropriate, either as a portent of additional doom or as a prelude to eternal enlightenment.

Grandfather meanwhile sat solid as a rock – his forecast having reached fruition – and I sat as solid as I could beside him. I was – did I realize it at the time? – sitting in the midst of the highest improbability, of that moment that brings together the past and the present and the future, all of time illustrated and documented, my own life and the lives of everyone else, including Grandfather's, no more than a second in the timeless mind of God but lives nonetheless worth extending into eternity if only we listened and responded to what Sister Hook was saying.

She was saying – shouting, actually, because the wind and the thunder and the pellets against the tent top were impressively competitive – that before Jehovah establishes his final kingdom there shall be a battle, the king of all battles, and it shall be called Armageddon. And what I remember above all else about this battle – excluding Sister Hook's rendition of it on the unfurling scroll, a rendition that Pablo Picasso surely would have drooled over – is that some sort of dam at last will break, *dam* being perhaps a metaphor I didn't understand, and blood would flow against a multitude of horses' fetlocks, would rise as the battle continues to touch the horses' bellies, would continue to rise to tarnish the silver on the bits of the horses' bridles, would . . .

Then, as suddenly almost as it had begun, the rain stopped and so too the lightning, and the thunder drifted away to a distant gurgling, then moved on into absolute silence. Sister Hook paused, looked heavenward then into the silent and inscrutable canvas that was the tent top. It took her only a few moments, I believe, to grasp inscrutability's elusive meaning: If Mother Nature had seen fit to lower her voice, then Sister Hook should see fit to lower hers, too.

And she did, and though she spoke in a subdued voice, almost a whisper, I could hear her as clearly as if she had been standing right beside me. She dropped Armageddon like the heavy burden it had become and, free of its awful weight, moved into what she called a Trinity of Christian Certainties.

Certainty Number One: The flames of hell are too hot ever to be imagined. They shall have been placed in hell by a God who cannot be mocked, by a jealous God who shall have no other gods before Him. To dramatize this initial certainty Sister Hook first pointed the tip of the catalpa branch at several of the red blotches that decorated her scroll. Then, as if her own paintings were not sufficient evidence, she laid her Bible on a chair near the pulpit, took a cigarette lighter from a pocket sewn into the flowered bedsheet, her dress, and lit it with a flick of her thumb, whereupon, waiting until the flame had steadied itself, she walked the lighter slowly and steadily, almost gracefully, to where her loyal servant stood holding the far end of the evangelist's remarkable scroll. That end had been attached to what looked like the handle of a rake or a broom, and the steadfast menial had been rolling the scroll onto this handle as Sister Hook explained the many ins and outs of man's sojourn on earth – and, I assumed, beyond.

Soon enough I came to appreciate the depth of the subaltern's devotion because, holding the end of the scroll with one hand, he passed the other hand deliberately over the flame, then back, then over again, each time lowering the hand until, behold, it barely moved at all, and I watched the man's flour-white face until it erupted in a scream that very nearly toppled even my grandfather.

Certainty Number Two: Eternity – and that's the span of time the unrepentant can expect to spend in hell – lasts a long, long time. Again, Sister Hook used the catalpa branch to draw our attention to the scroll, but this time to the scroll in general, to its grandiose sweep of eons, not to specific elements within the eons. Then with a homely analogy she attempted to illustrate that eternity lasts, as she had said, for a long, long time. She chose wheat to serve as the lynchpin for her analogy – or, more precisely, one single solitary grain of wheat, trillions of which, she said, are harvested yearly here in God's vast and fertile breadbasket. Now imagine, she said, all of those grains of wheat – in their various bins all around not only Kansas but all around the heartland, and not only in bins but also in elevators, and not only in elevators but on the ground, all those grains that the machines failed to glean or, in the gleaning, somehow dropped – imagine all of those grains of wheat being carried away, one grain at a time, by, say, a meadowlark that carries away only one grain every one hundred years. Imagine how long it would take for the meadowlark to carry away one thimbleful of wheat, how long it would take for the bird to fill a calf bucket, a washtub, a cattle tank. Imagine, then, that having filled a calf bucket or a washtub or a cattle tank the bird would have lived no more than one second of eternity's lifetime.

I was trying to imagine all of this, but I kept drifting into snags. I could imagine a meadowlark because each summer we had meadowlarks on fence posts only a few yards from our house; and I could imagine the wheat, in bins and elevators and lying in fields of stubble, because my father as a hired hand often drove a combine, and sometimes he took me with him – not for an entire day but maybe for a round or two after lunch, after mother and the other women had delivered sandwiches and cold drinks. But I couldn't imagine all that wheat waiting to be carried off by a single bird; other birds would have eaten the grains on the ground, and the wheat in the bins and in the elevators would have been long sold and carried away by trains to wherever it goes when it goes away.

So I pretty much gave up on trying to imagine the magnitude of eternity and instead focused on the antics of Sister Hook. She had taken up her Bible from the chair near the pulpit and was using it to approximate the meadowlark as, with this approximation extended by one arm, she approximated the bird's flight with her tiptoe movements back and forth across the platform. She was as graceful, I suppose, as a very large evangelist can hope to be, but I nonetheless expected that at any moment either the bird or its carrier might fall, and I was concerned. All during this phase of the triad I sat on the edge of my chair, my eyes probably wide, my mouth probably open, awaiting the fall, which, thank God, never happened.

Certainty Number Three: The eternal flames of hell can be avoided only by the confessing of sins and the accepting of Jesus Christ as the one and only Savior. For some time now Sister Hook's delivery had been *sotto voce*; but with the mentioning of Jesus Christ as the one and only Savior, the evangelist could no longer abide restraint. Having nodded to her accomplice, who unfurled the scroll to reveal its final depiction – the haloed face of Jesus – Sister Hook exploded into song: *I will sing of my Redeemer, of His wondrous love to me; on the cruel cross He suffered, from the curse to set me free. . . .* With her free hand Sister Hook punished her Bible as if somehow it had offended her, and her movements on the platform were no longer attempts at birdlike delicacy. She paced, and the deliberate beat of her pacing must have given the band its cue, for it began to play with considerable gusto. *Sing, oh sing, of my Redeemer, with His blood He purchased me; on the cross He sealed my pardon, paid the debt, and made me free. . . .*

I looked at Grandfather. Was he smiling? To this day, I do not know how he lost that quarter section of decent land just north of town, and probably I will never know. My father didn't know, either, though he said that he believed the man who housed my grandfather's wheat, the man who owned the local elevator, was a crook, and I believed this, too, because my father said it. Even so, there were loose ends that I wanted to see tied up; I wanted to know, once and for all, that my grandfather's move to an inferior quarter section near Cedar Vale had been a choice forced upon him by a crook.

Now the aisle was busy with folks moving toward the altar, Sister Hook having played what surely must have been her trump card: *Changed, changed, in the twinkling of an eye – changed, changed, in the twinkling of an eye; the trumpet shall sound, the dead shall be raised, changed in the twinkling of an eye!* Several times she had emphasized how quickly the change would occur, that shift from this world into the next, a change that would happen too rapidly for anyone to make any last-moment move in the direction of salvation. So make the move now, Sister Hook said, or you might not ever have another chance. As Sister Hook sang and exhorted, the band had provided an impressive backup, especially the trumpets – *the trumpet shall sound, the dead shall be raised*. But when she moved into a softer invitation, the band went silent: *Softly and tenderly Jesus is calling, calling for you and for me; O see at the portals He's watching and waiting, waiting for you and for me. . . .*

We did not stay to watch the end of the service. We did stay long enough, however, for me to hear some howlings and some language that I could not decipher. *Glos-so-la-lia.* I knew neither word nor concept. *Tongues.* I knew the word, but not the word as later I'd hear it in the phrase *speaking in tongues.* It had something to do with fire igniting the tongues of the saved and *sanc-ti-fied* and with the Holy Spirit visiting some of the biblically chosen to inspire their peculiar words.

We walked down the aisle to the back of the tent, then stepped outside. And oh how sweet, how fresh the air! I had not realized how stuffy the inside of the tent, with its flaps down, had become; but now, in the open air, a richness of mild breeze and of earthiness returned me to fecundity, to my little brother wriggling his toes in the ooze on the floor of our hand-dug cave.

About halfway between the big tent and our Chevrolet, Grandfather stopped. At first I thought he might be stopping to relieve himself, as he often did on the farm, but he made no move in that direction. Instead, he looked up at the sky, probably wondering if more rain was likely to fall. I looked up, too, but there was not a cloud anywhere to be seen – nothing but vastness, and stars by the thousands wanting to fill it. I tried to locate the Big Dipper but couldn't, then tried to find the Pleiades, but I couldn't find them either.

Last year at school an Indian had talked to us about stories, and told some stories of his own, and one of them I could remember very clearly. The Indian's name was Little Horse; he was a Kiowa, he said, and the story he told, the one that I best remember, was about a Kiowa family that many, many winters ago, before the white man arrived in his country, lived in northern Oklahoma. The mother and father had eight children – one boy and seven girls. The boy, who was the oldest, loved to tease his little sisters; he especially liked to frighten them. So he would surprise them by jumping suddenly from his hiding place among the bushes or behind a tree and, pretending to hold a bow and an arrow, would chase them, pretending to shoot them with his imaginary weapon.

But his favorite way to frighten the girls was to pretend that he was a bear. He had a strong voice, and a low one, too, and he could make a sound exactly like the ferocious growling of a bear. The growling was so convincing that the girls would never fail to please him by screaming and running away.

One day the boy, pretending to be a bear, was chasing his frightened sisters when he noticed that fur was beginning to grow on his arms – and it was growing very quickly, and it was spreading to his legs and to his neck, and with his furry hands he could feel thick fur already covering his face. The boy was amazed and fearful, but when he saw that his sisters had turned their heads to see how close behind them he was and that they had seen the fur on his body and thus were screaming and running more distractedly than ever, his fear turned to delight: This time he would frighten his silly sisters nearly to death!

The girls ran and ran, staying as close together as possible, until they reached a grove of trees, where they made a half circle, then another, hoping to lose the bear that once had been their brother. When they could run no longer they stopped beside the sawed-off stump of what once had been a very large tree. They were breathing heavily. They listened closely. For a minute or two they heard nothing; then one of them said, Listen! I think I can hear him coming!

Yes, they could hear him – a low, distant growl, but slowly the

43

growl was becoming louder. Then, out of nowhere, they heard a voice: Jump on my back, it said, and I will save you!

The girls could not believe their ears. They looked around. They could see no one. But they could hear the growling of their brother who was now a bear coming closer.

They were holding each other tightly when again they heard the voice from nowhere: Jump on my back, it said, and I will save you!

One of the girls looked down at the surface of the stump.

The stump has spoken, she said. Follow me!

And the girl jumped onto the surface of the stump, whereupon the other sisters jumped on the tree stump, too. When the last of the sisters was standing on the stump, it began slowly to rise. The growling of the brother grew louder and louder, but the stump continued to rise until the bear, having arrived at the tree, could not reach its sisters, no matter how fiercely it growled or how savagely it clawed at the tree's thick bark. And the stump continued to rise; higher and higher it rose, and it was rising still as the sun went down and darkness covered the earth where the girls had been. When at last the stump stopped rising, the sisters stepped off to find themselves at their new home in the sky. And, said Little Horse, we know them today as the Pleiades, the Seven Sisters. They are safe now for eternity in the heavens.

We walked to the Chevrolet without saying anything, the sounds of the revival becoming more remote, more subdued. When I took my seat in the car beside my grandfather, I could barely hear anything at all, and the big tent – what I could see of it through the many slender trunks of the catalpas – didn't appear all that big.

Our Chevrolet took us through an expanse of muddy stubble without a hitch. All the way home I left the window down. I could still smell the sawdust and the woodchips, some of them at the edges of the tent having been soaked, when we pulled into the gravel driveway.

4

MY FASCINATION WITH ROCKS began at an early age, though I am not certain how early. Probably its beginning, like most of my other beginnings, could be traced back to Sunday school and church, where more than seventy times seven we forgave ourselves and where we sang about rocks in "Rock of Ages" and *Jesus is the rock in a weary land, a weary land, a weary land; Oh Jesus is the rock in a weary land, a shelter in the time of storm.* Most, if not all, of the rock songs were reassuring – the rock as a place to hide (from brothers, say, who would be bears) or as a symbol of strength for those who were weak and exhausted.

Then came the rocks that infested my grandfather's farm near Cedar Vale, the one he probably bought for a song after he had lost the other farm to a crook. These rocks ranged in size from pebbles to boulders, and they could be viewed from more than one perspective. Grandfather saw them, collectively, as a perpetual nuisance if not in fact an ongoing threat. To give his little plots of wheat and lespedeza a chance to survive, he would harness his team and, horses pulling a grain wagon, would scour the fields, lifting those rocks that could be lifted into the wagon, cursing – but ever so mildly and never any curse from the heart – those rocks too large for even a large, sweet, stubborn German to lift.

If one such rock, however, lay in the path of necessary progress, Grandfather would find a way to move it, as he did the boulder that resided squarely in the middle of the driveway, a long, narrow stretch that meandered upward from the gravel road in the valley to the south to the farmhouse at the side of a rocky hill. I watched him affix a contraption of ropes and chains and baling wire to this boulder; watched him use a small cable to affix this contraption to a hitch on a singletree; watched then as his obedient horses tugged and strained and broke wind until, behold, the boulder moved, then moved some more; watched as the horses, inspired no doubt by Grandfather's words of encouragement, doubled their effort and with one final and glorious surge took that immense rock well beyond the side of the driveway, where on a half acre of bunchgrass it came to rest and where it probably rests today – and where (I am guessing) it will spend eternity.

On the other hand, if the boulder lay in a place merely inconvenient, and if the lower portion of its bulk extended Lord-only-knows-how-deeply into the ground, Grandfather would leave it alone. He learned over the years to abide these rocks, to live with them, to plow and to plant around them: To say there is always the rock, he said, with actions if not with words, is not to forfeit the harvest.

Not that he ever had much of a harvest to forfeit, even during the most favorable season. His quarter section was essentially the side of a long hill that began its serious tapering heavenward immediately west of the house; that acreage east of the house tapered downward, hellward, but more gradually, which meant that this was the land most suitable for plowing and planting. Both of the taperings, though, were infested with rocks.

Or if not *in-fes-ted*, then decorated, at least as perceived by me and my brother; from the beginning, from the first time we saw this hilly, gumbooed, rock-dominated chunk of real estate, we thought we had died and gone to the flip side of Sister Hook's Inferno. No streets paved with gold, certainly, and no cherubs sitting on clouds of cumulus playing harps and singing, say, "The Old Rugged Cross." Nothing but scrub pine and bunchgrass and a hill that reached halfway to the Seven Sisters – and rocks, rocks, rocks. Rocks to hide behind. Rocks to ascend. Rocks to roll over, if we could, to open a moist universe of critters. And rocks to ride.

It lay just east of the farmhouse, and all who saw it said that, yes, it looked precisely like a turtle – like a turtle's back, anyway, and a turtle's head and even a turtle's tail, the back of the rock tapering suddenly to form an appendage that indeed looked to be an honest-to-goodness turtle's tail. The rock was large enough to accommodate both my little brother and me, and we spent many hours atop its back, riding neither rock nor turtle, but a saddleless pony that took us wherever we wanted to go and that delivered us from enemies too numerous and too God-awful to recount. On other occasions we took turns riding the rock, going it alone, and at other times – and these were the most exciting – we rode the rock at night, backgrounded by the grunting of Grandfather's hogs, overhead the Big Dipper and a half moon lighting the barbs on the barbwire fence that encircled the cows and the horses.

Was I too old to be riding a rock? Perhaps. I was ten, I believe, and my brother was eight, and I was large for my size, as my mother said, and my brother, for his size, was small. Maybe as the larger and older brother I wanted to encourage his imagination, maybe my own pleasure derived from being a part of my brother's pleasure, or maybe – and perhaps this is the most likely – I rode the rock because it was fun being both cowhand and magician, not water into wine but rock into pony, boy presto-change-o into man.

Epiphanies come in a myriad of sizes and shapes. When the Almighty informed Mary that she was to have a child without benefit of a mortal man's cooperation, she must have experienced an epiphany of the highest order. When Jesus, not long after arising from the dead, the stone that sealed his tomb having been rolled away, stone perhaps as large as the one Grandfather's horses removed from the driveway, told his disciples that he would see them later, those disciples must have felt something cold as an icicle move up their collective spine. Call it an epiphany. And when on several occasions Athena spoke to her favorite mortal, Odysseus, that great adventurous soul must have experienced, with each dialogue, a distinctive tingling worthy of the name *epiphany*.

But not all dialogues occur on such a lofty level. Most of them, perhaps alas, are more pedestrian.

Such was the dialogue my brother and I experienced with Turtle Rock, and with elements beyond the rock. On clear early evenings, riding the rock, we spoke with the hush that was the evening, with the sounds of the evening and with its farmyard aromas, that blend of horse and cow and cows' milk and soil despoiled and enriched by hogs and chickens; what we saw and inhaled and touched, that cool flank of the cool pony we rode on, these were the words that constituted the dialogue that in the red-letter edition of our lives remain in red.

And forty-some years later, when I suggested to my brother that we return to the farm to find Turtle Rock to perhaps bring it to Nebraska to plant it in my backyard, he quickly agreed.

We located the farm easily enough, though it was no longer *the* farm. It belonged to someone else, and its buildings, except for the granary, had been leveled – the henhouse and the lean-to for the horses and cattle leveled by age, no doubt, and the garage and the house brought to their knees by fire; a number of charred boards told us that someone with matches, perhaps the owner himself, had paid these vestiges of my grandfather's farm a final visit.

It took us a while to locate Turtle Rock – so long, in fact, that we were at the edge of giving up. Then we saw it, sitting on a space we had neglected because each of us knew that the rock resided elsewhere.

We were not surprised that finally we found the rock, but we were surprised to see that it was as large as we remembered it, and that it did indeed so clearly resemble a turtle. We looked at it and admired it and walked around it, and in my mind's bluest eye I tried to picture it sitting in my backyard in Nebraska – somewhere between the two walnut trees, perhaps – but for some reason the image refused to focus.

When at last I bent over to lift one end of the turtle to test its weight I learned for myself what Grandfather ages ago had learned: Some rocks are not meant to be relocated. I didn't learn this instantaneously; I learned it when my brother's helping hand did nothing at all to help – Turtle Rock didn't budge.

We stood up, my brother and I, and looked at each other with – there is no other word – astonishment. My little brother had outgrown his littleness when he was a senior in high school; almost overnight he had grown both up and out, and now, one ice age later, he stood near Turtle Rock a full-blown man, and I, likewise full-blown, stood less than an arm's length from him.

My brother smiled and shook his head. I smiled and nodded my agreement. Ours was a mutual understanding, an acknowledgment that, though we were both full-blown, we were not going to take this rock anywhere – not without the aid of our grandfather's horses, and they were no longer available, their wide, muscled haunches having many seasons ago gone on to greener pastures.

But boys will be boys, as they say, so we attempted a compromise, meaning that with an old fencepost we would try to move the rock just enough to let it know that we had been there. The fencepost, of course, broke cleanly at that spot where we had placed a small stone as a fulcrum. We tried another post, but it broke, too, and at the same spot.

We need something stronger than a rotten fencepost, my brother said.

I said, Yes. We need something stronger.

The day was warm but not too warm, and there was an easy breeze coming to us from the south-southwest. Less than an hour earlier we had eaten gooberburgers at the Tacoma Gooberburger in Cedar Vale. We therefore had nothing better to do than look for a lever stronger than a rotten fencepost.

Johnny found one, a modern-day fencepost in the form of a steel rod with hooks near one end to help keep it in the ground. He took it to Turtle Rock and, having asked me to call him hereafter Archimedes, forced the hook end of the rod into the ground against the rock, then placed the fulcrum where he anticipated it might be most useful when we began again the business of applying leverage.

We applied the leverage slowly, and finally full-blown, until Turtle Rock, behold, budged, and the lever, behold, bent like a wet noodle.

My brother, standing, said, She budged.

I agreed.

We left the rock then, with the two generations of fenceposts beside it, and serpentined our way down a driveway now populated thickly with weeds back in the direction of the car. Both of us, I believe, had resigned ourselves to accepting what the god of rocks so mightily dictated. More than resigned, we were, I further believe, almost elated – because we had been defeated, and thus humbled, and had accepted both with a grin and a shrug, an acceptance that kicked the possibility of undue pride squarely in its haughty ass-end.

Ralph Waldo Emerson had something to say about all of this, or at least some of it, in his poem "Each and All." Did I remember this poem as I walked with my brother down the driveway toward the car? Probably not. But chronology has at best a habit of collapsing, of becoming quickly smaller, like the leaky bellows of the old red-and-black accordion as my grandfather squeezed it, or at worst not frankly giving a damn. So remembering the poem now is the equivalent of having remembered it several years ago. Perhaps.

In his poem Emerson contends that "Nothing is fair or good alone," then goes on to illustrate his point with three examples, each of which suggests that not only is nothing fair or good alone but that each element in nature, including the human one, does its best work, looks its best and sounds its purest note, when it occupies that place most appropriate to its essence. The poet removes a sparrow, for instance, from its alder bough and takes it home only to discover that, away from the river and the open sky, the bird sings no longer to the poet's eye but only to his ear. Then, apparently wanting more evidence to support his thesis, Emerson takes home some "delicate shells" from the seashore:

> *The delicate shells lay on the shore;*
> *The bubbles of the latest wave*
> *Fresh pearls to their enamel gave,*
> *And the bellowing of the savage sea*
> *Greeted their safe escape to me.*
> *I wiped away the weeds and foam,*
> *I fetched my sea-born treasures home;*
> *But the poor, unsightly, noisome things*

Had left their beauty on the shore
With the sun and the sand and the wild uproar.

Diction and syntax, meter and rhyme to the contrary notwithstanding, this is a good poem, because what it says is that my brother and I had no business removing Turtle Rock from its natural habitat, and probably that is why, earlier, I had not been able to clearly imagine Turtle Rock resting in my backyard in Nebraska. In my backyard there were no fellow boulders for it to hobnob with, no hill to serve as a backdrop, and no chickens to peck at its edges for beetles and bugs. On a rainy night my backyard, with its ryegrass mowed low, harbored plenty of night crawlers, and often I would go with my sons and a flashlight to catch them until their slick writhing bodies filled a Folgers can, but there were no hogs grunting as we snatched up the crawlers, no calf bawling for its mother, no barbwire for the moon to glint the barbs of.

Halfway down the narrow road my brother stopped to tell me that he could eat another gooberburger. Because my brother has an appetite, this did not surprise me. A gooberburger, incidentally, is a hamburger laced liberally with peanut butter. It is disarmingly tasty, especially if washed down with a peanut butter malt. To humor my brother I told him that I could eat another gooberburger, too.

Then I saw, not more than thirty feet to the right, the boulder that had lost its tug-of-war with Grandfather's tandem of horses. There it sat, precisely where it should have been sitting, huge and patient and important and, not altogether unlike the rest of us, acting immortal.

5

WHEN THE HOTSHOT BUSINESSMAN from Wichita, having finished his hot roast beef sandwich in my parents' cafe, asked my father to manage one of his ranches, a twelve-hundred-acre spread between Sharon and Kiowa, and my father, behold, accepted, I was less excited than afraid. My father had no experience as a rancher; he had dropped out of school after the sixth grade to help my grandfather on the acreage north of Attica, my town, and several years later, having met the woman of his dreams, my mother, he left the farm and became a utility handyman, then a small-time entrepreneur, then many years later a janitor at a lumberyard, a third-shift job that he held until age eighty-two, when, on a clear, bright Sunday afternoon, a drunk driver broadsided both him and his old brown Dodge into a blood-soaked oblivion.

Ah, but the ranch, as it turned out, was a sweet, sweet place for a young man who had been raised in the city, who at a tender age had heard the sound of pool balls clicking, who had had his hair cut and trimmed by a man who in secret sipped whiskey in the back of his shop, and who had experienced the deliberate thrill of dizziness as he stood on a platform at the railroad station as a freight the size of Armageddon rumbled by.

Ah, but the ranch! It was vast and, I believed, unexplored, and there were ponies for me and my brother to ride to do the exploring. The ponies were so tame and so friendly that, seeing me and my brother approaching, they would bow their heads in anticipation of the bridles. We rode bareback, as we had turtle rock, over the green undulations of pasture grass, urging the milk cows to the barn and into the stanchions where my father, with the help of me and my brother and the hired hand, fit the milkers to the cows' teats and stood back to watch and listen as the magic milkers did their work.

But when we were not herding milk cows we were exploring,

and what we found on our first expedition was a treasure lying clean and multitudinous on the tops of small, grass-free knolls all across the pasture.

Rocks!

Pebbles, actually, all of them, all fifty or so million, rain-washed and ready to be fired from our slingshots. Praise the Lord, I might have said, and pass the ammunition!

Because a war was going on and everyone back in the city had been talking about it, my buddies, including of course R. D., were up to their chins in patriotic zeal, and for good reason: The Allies were turning the tables on the Axis powers. Sugar and gas rationing were paying off; Lucky Strike green had gone to war, and Lucky Strike green, whatever that might have been, was winning. Adolph Hitler, with his comic mustache and his belief in a god whose favorite color was white, was maybe about to arise one morning with egg on his face: *Isn't this old Hitler's face? Yes, sir, Hitler's face! Isn't it a damned disgrace? Yes, sir, a damned disgrace!* We city boys had heard that song in the pool hall or the filling station or the drugstore and, having heard it, repeated it, all of it, including *damned*, at every opportunity. We had been told that loose lips sink ships, but apparently that did not apply to songs that denigrated the big bad three – Adolph Hitler, Tojo, Mussolini:

> *Tramp, tramp, tramp, the boys are marching;*
> *now they're standing at the door.*
> *If I had a tommygun, I would make old Tojo run,*
> *and he'd never Yankee Doodle any more!*

If I had a tommygun! Yes, or a rocket launcher or flamethrower or MI or Bangalore torpedo or hand grenade or a cheesy chunk of trinitrotoluene! Jesus, what I couldn't do with a handful of TNT wouldn't be worth doing. Do you read me, Adolph? Tojo? Mussolini?

In the pool hall one afternoon our local undertaker, Ora Brant, asked the pool sharks and the domino players to take a break while he read them the following: *To a people that pass successfully through these trials ordained by Providence, the Almighty will give in the end the laurel wreath of victory and, thus, the prize of life.* When he looked up the players, to a man, were applauding, after which Brant told them who the author was: Adolph Hitler.

Well, I had no TNT nor did any of my city buddies nor did my two closest country buddies, Willie and Ralphie Robinson, who had their own ranch a mile and a half north. They were identical red-headed twins with identical gaps between their identical front upper teeth, and when they weren't spitting through those teeth or manufacturing perfume – about which I'll say more later – they were assembling slingshots, assembling them against that day when they might be called upon to use them against Hitler, Tojo, Mussolini.

My brother and I weren't dummies; we too knew how to put together a slingshot, how to scrounge the rubber from an old innertube, how to scrounge a small rectangle of leather from the tongue of a discarded shoe or boot, how with string to affix the strands of rubber to the Y of a small tree branch, how with additional string to secure the leather to the rubber strands. We knew all of this. We were city boys. We had cut our teeth in the alleys and on the highways and the byways of a town whose grocery store, owned by the Moultons, sometimes stayed open until midnight on Saturday.

It is not surprising, then, that when my brother and I saw the unending mounds of perfectly sized ammunition we almost wet our overalls in brotherly unison. I looked at my brother, who was looking at me. We nodded – I believe in unison – and then having dismounted, we walked to where the cache lay atop its knoll and kneeling, in unison, we lifted pebble after pebble to know its heft and texture, and surely our actions, and the grace with which we handled the pebbles, must have constituted a form of prayer: *God is great. God is good. Let us thank Him for this.* . . .

It did not take us all day to decide what to do: scrounge containers of any and all descriptions and fill them with rocks – against that day when we might be called upon to use them against Hitler, Tojo, Mussolini.

Believe this much: An obsession can be a sword with more than one edge. It can be thrilling, on the one hand, to have a mission, to believe that what you are doing goes above and beyond your own petty concerns. Thus, as we scrounged containers, mostly discarded calf buckets that lay scattered like rusted afterthoughts around the acreage, and filled those containers with rocks that ached, we knew, to feel the soft leather that formed the pocket of the slingshot, we sensed that what we were doing was being compelled and directed by a higher power, that we were moving toward a consummation that would finally yield, for me and my brother and for all mankind, the laurel wreath of victory.

We hid our containers, filled to overflowing with ammunition, in the southwest corner of the haymow, covering them with loose hay concealed by a wall of bales. We would be ready, by God, when the time came.

But the time didn't come, and therein lies one of the other edges of the sword. How many buckets of ammunition should you stash before stopping? How much, finally, is enough? It is not easy to stop something whose momentum is considerable and whose cause is just and noble. If we were never called upon to use the rocks against our enemies, perhaps the act of stashing them would be enough for us to claim our fair share of glory when the enemies surrendered. Isn't the thought sometimes equal to the deed? In Sunday school I had been told that sometimes it is, though I do not believe that my teacher had the storing of rocks in mind when she explained, or tried to explain, that invisible and sometimes nonexistent line between the deed and the thought.

So we collected rocks and stored them until one day Willie and Ralphie Robinson told us that barn swallows were the enemy. My brother and I, though street smart, had never thought of barn swallows as the enemy, and when Willie and Ralphie told us that barn swallows were Stukas and Zeros and Messerschmitts somehow transmogrified, as it were, to resemble birds, my brother and I were mortified. How could we have been so innocent, so naive, so outright blind? Probably the answer lies in our obsession with the gathering of rocks, with our storing of ammunition, with a compulsive desire to have more and more of what already we had more than enough of.

Willie and Ralphie, pausing frequently to spit stoutly through the identical gaps in their identical teeth, told us further how to confront this enemy: At dusk watch for the feathered planes to fly into the haymow, by way of an open haymow door, then, when the rafters are filled with so-called birds, slip softly up the haymow stairs and close the haymow door, whereupon, having filled your pockets with so-called rocks, use your flashlight to pinpoint and confuse a so-called swallow and with your slingshot – call it an MI or a launcher – fire at the enemy until the enemy is brought down.

Jesus. Willie and Ralphie, red-headed country boys, were wiser than ever we had imagined.

Thereafter for many nights my brother and I brought down the imposters, he holding the flashlight during one sortie, I holding it during another, we having managed to assemble a launcher sufficient unto each bringing-down.

These nights, individually and collectively, constitute the final and most bothersome edge on the blade of that cockeyed, tri-edged sword. Because there was something haunting and uncanny about this business of killing Germans and Japs, something slightly off center, as if our self-deception was working to reduce the ranks of the enemy but not working to convince my brother and me that our cause was either just or noble. Yet we persisted. Night after night we trapped the birds and brought down two or three; night after night we tossed their corpses into a dead space between the barn and the tool shed – sustenance and playthings for the cats and coyotes.

I don't know much about barn swallows, except that their flight is erratic – they can rise and dip and change directions almost too quickly for the human eye to follow, like their cousins the cliff swallows and their nephews the bridge swallows – and at dusk they can rather easily be hoodwinked into believing that an open haymow door is an invitation to safety and a good night's sleep. They are dark-feathered, lovely creatures, I know that much, and when confronted with the beam of a flashlight they become confused, or so it seems – to fly or not to fly? – and by the time they have made a decision, it is too late and the pebbles sink into their soft breasts and they fall into the hay without so much as a whisper.

Haunting and uncanny, a blend of the sweet and the sour – because a haymow at night exudes a feel and an aroma too distinct not to be taken in and remembered. Hay, loose and baled; air not moving, air filled with motes uncountable animated by the beam of the flashlight; traces of milk and mash and manure rising from a long file of stanchions. How all of this provides a premonition that is almost palpable so that when the first rock ricochets, *ric-o-chets*, off the rafters, the sound is a shellshock to the system, regardless of how well prepared the system believes itself to be. Sometimes the rock will glance off a rafter to strike the underside of the roof to ricochet then to strike another rafter, or maybe a strut, each instant of contact as if an echo of what preceded it, until the final sound is that of a single drumbeat at the bottom of a deep, inverted canyon.

Sooner or later, of course, one of the rocks would not ricochet, would instead find a German or a Jap and the contrastive silence provided by the direct hit would startle almost as much as would the ricocheting. And my brother and I would add another notch to the handle of our slingshot.

And the ritual occurred, with its sweet and sour undertones, until our older sister, Bernadine, discovered what we were doing. She told her mother, who in turn told her husband, who in turn told his sons to stop killing the swallows or he would kick their little asses up somewhere between their shoulder blades – or words to that effect.

Because our father's threat seemed to have come from the heart, my brother and I retired our slingshots and moved almost immediately into a business that we hoped, if not assumed, would make each of us a millionaire.

Willie and Ralphie had invented the perfume and when at recess one day they showed the tiny bottle to me and told me to remove the lid and smell the contents, I did so strictly out of a sense of curiosity. Well, the contents did indeed smell like perfume, like my sister smelled sometimes on a Sunday morning when we lived in the city and went to Sunday school.

It smells pretty good, I said.

We made it ourselves, Ralphie said. Willie nodded.

And we can make more of it, said Willie. Ralphie nodded.

And we can sell it, Ralphie said. And make money, added Willie.

Eventually I came to understand that the Robinson twins had hit onto a formula for the manufacturing of a perfume that might well make them rich. And they were willing, they said, to share the wealth with me and my brother, providing we buy into the company with some up-front cash. I told them I'd have to think about it.

I thought about it that night – and so did my brother, to whom I had confided the twins' offer, whereupon my brother said, But we're broke.

We were indeed broke. But after thinking about it that night, and most of the next day, we decided to confront the Robinson boys with something in lieu of cash: instructions for the building of a slinger.

The twins, behold, nodded yes. Our instructions for the building of a slinger even up for the twins' recipe for perfume. We shook hands.

My brother looked at me and winked. We knew that the two red-headed country boys loved their slingshots and that they loved to use them and that they had no sister to tattle on them or a father who felt so keenly about the demise of swallows that he would kick their little asses somewhere up between their shoulder blades, or words to that effect, should they shoot them; so we assumed that the twins would be eager to learn how to put together another weapon so that they might expand their destruction. What we didn't know, and thus worried over, was whether they already knew how to build a slinger.

They didn't. So I led them along, telling them that the slinger was a secret weapon and that therefore not very many people knew about it – certainly not the Germans or the Japs – until their identical blue eyes told me that they were more than willing, they were downright eager, to swap formulas.

Then Ralphie said, Don't *tell* us how to make the slinger. *Show* us.

We spent the day putting together a slinger. We found a suitable limb, dead but not brittle, on one of the Robinson trees in a shelter-belt north of the house, a limb approximately three feet long with a diameter of maybe one inch. Near one end I used my Barlow to carve a groove into which I wound a string, tying it off with three half hitches, a knot illustrated clearly in the *Boy Scout Handbook*, my copy of which I had lost when we made the move to the ranch between Sharon and Kiowa.

The Robinson twins studied each of my movements as if memorizing documents that, once committed to memory, must be burned or swallowed. They were tough, no-nonsense young men, yet they were generous, too (hadn't they been willing to share their secret formula, their impending millions?), and they smiled a lot and laughed, too, and the spit they sent like the tails of comets through the identical gaps in their identical teeth sometimes found its mark. And never did I see one twin spit without the other twin following suit. It was bingo-bingo, and if the first bingo missed its target the second might hit it dead center.

Now we had a limb, I believe cottonwood, with a string attached to one end. The twins studied me as I went to the other end of the string to tie several knots to form a dollop approximately four times the size of the BB that had struck my buddy R. D. almost in the eye.

I paused then to remove my Barlow from a front pocket in my overalls. I opened the blade to feel its edge with my thumb. The twins, who owned pocket knives of their own, nonetheless studied me. I was pausing because I knew that the final item necessary to the completion of the deadly slinger would not be easy to find.

Now, I said, we need a shingle.

The Robinson boys looked at each other and nodded identically to each other.

64

Follow us, they said.

We followed them to the Robinson henhouse, a building comprised of a long, low series of coops with wire mesh fronts and a roof covered with well-weathered shingles. Ralphie made a cradle with his hands, and Willie soon was atop the henhouse, where in less time than it takes to tell it he had found a loose shingle. He handed me the shingle, then stood back to begin again the studying.

With the Barlow I split the shingle down the middle, then split one of the sections again, leaving me a length of shingle approximately two inches wide. I could almost feel the twins' eyes at my hands as I worked very slowly to carve out an arrow, leaving three inches of the thin end of the shingle as the arrow's feather, then whittling away the soft cedar to form a shaft about the size of either Ralphie's or Willie's index finger, they being identical. By now the Robinson boys must surely have deduced that I was making an arrow, but their intensity never wavered.

I went about the shaping of the arrow very meticulously, not only because I wanted to impress the country boys but also out of necessity – because a shingle is a light and delicate thing and one slip of the Barlow might wound the arrow beyond recovery.

When I had the shaft appropriately pared down, I whittled its tip to a point, then halfway up the shaft I cut a notch in the shape of a very small check mark. I could sense that the twins were becoming increasingly anxious; spit was finding its way through their gapped teeth more and more regularly, and with their hands in their pockets they were inching closer and closer to where the expert was wielding his Barlow. From time to time the expert looked up to take note of their proximity.

When I had the notch shaved into its precise and necessary shape, I ran my fingers along the full length of the arrow. Yes, each of its parts seemed ready – feather, shaft, point, and the notch into which I would fit the knot at the end of the string when the time should arrive for liftoff.

Now the principal drawback to the slinger, as a weapon, is its infallible inaccuracy; it is simply not possible to hit anything what-soever with its arrow, unless by chance. Another drawback is that the arrow, being light and delicate, breaks easily when it comes into contact with anything denser than a mattress.

So when the time for liftoff seemed ripe, I told the Robinson boys to follow me, and I led them, my little brother beside me, to an expanse of pasture south of the Robinson homestead – nothing but rolling grassland beneath our feet, nothing but sky the color of un-washed denim over our heads. The nearest tree was a scrub oak per-haps half a day's ride in my grandfather's Chevy off to the west.

I chose as a launching site a flat piece of acreage at the base of a grassless knob where dozens of lovely and deadly rocks lay waiting. I ran the string of the slinger along the notch until the knot at the end of the string checked its movement; then, holding the base of the limb in my right hand and the feather of the arrow between the thumb and index finger of my left hand, being careful to keep the string taut, I swept the weapon slowly to my left, as if cocking some sort of prehistoric rifle, then in one mighty and feral motion I launched the arrow upward.

How in the name of all that is just and honorable is it not pos-sible to be pleased with perfection? The arrow sped upward until it reached the nearest stratosphere, then, encouraged by its own suc-cess, it seemed to increase its velocity until it had punctured the next stratosphere – and so on until it was out of sight, leaving me and my little brother and Willie and Ralphie Robinson blinking like half-blinded and bemused owls into the blue bottomless bowl of an ear-ly August afternoon.

When the arrow finally returned to earth it found a clump of bunchgrass to lose its point in, a clump not more than twenty feet away. Willie and Ralphie were so impressed that for more than a minute or two they had neglected to spit.

I walked to the arrow and removing it from the bunchgrass I walked it back to where the twins were identically standing. When I gave them first the arrow, then the slinger, they accepted each with a humility that miracles just naturally give rise to. And I believe I know what they were thinking: With this new weapon we shall be able to destroy more swallows, more enemy, than anyone can ever shake a stick at.

I didn't tell them about the weapon's shortcomings. I would let them discover these failings – poor misguided bloodthirsty country creatures – for themselves.

For the record, my father, upon learning that Johnny and I were helping the war effort by bringing down Germans and Japanese camouflaged as barn swallows, did not threaten to kick our little asses up somewhere between our shoulder blades. That's an expression I would hear after we moved back to town. What he said was more like, Stop shooting those birds – or I might have to tan your hides. My father knew how to curse, yes, and how to lay on a curse, but never did he curse me or my brother and never did he lay a hand on either of us.

Even so, there was an intensity in his voice that told me he meant what he said. So, as I mentioned earlier, I stopped contributing to the war effort, and of course my brother, though not my twin, stopped also.

And believe this much: I felt better. And the reason is that I managed to figure out why our shooting the swallows wasn't altogether satisfying, in spite of their detestable allegiances.

It was because barn swallows are not sparrows.

Sparrows, understand, are (1) plentiful in the extreme and (2) no more attractive than the common housefly. Barn swallows, on the other hand, are beautiful in their darkness and in the spontaneity of their erratic flight. And, too, barn swallows are not plentiful in the extreme. One can imagine the barn swallow by way of slingshots and other boyhood machinations being wiped out – and so, too, the robin, the dove, the lark, the oriole, the thrush, and so on – but one cannot imagine the absolute and utter demise of the sparrow. Can one?

The Robinson boys, not surprisingly, were true to their word: They gave me and my brother their formula for the making of a perfume that, mass produced, might well make all of us wealthy beyond our wildest dreams.

They told us that the formula was simple, to a point – some water in a jelly jar, a few drops from a lemon stirred into the water, and (and here's the catch) a teaspoon of what they called "powdered limestone."

We had no limestone on the Kloefkorn ranch, but on the Robinson spread were several beds of the white, soft stuff; Ralphie and Willie took us to one of these beds and showed us how to turn the limestone into powder: Hit the limestone with a hammer until it turns to a dry mush.

They performed this act of on-the-spot transmutation as I and my brother looked on, we being perhaps as rapt as were the twins when I assembled the slinger and carved the arrow. They had taken the jelly jar, with its water and its lemon and a lid to confine them, with them to the bed of soft white rock – and of course they had taken a hammer, too, an oversized ballpeen more than equal to whatever chunk of limestone. But they had not remembered to bring along a spoon, so Ralphie with an index finger did the stirring as Willie dropped what he guessed to be a spoonful of powdered limestone into the swirling water.

Ralphie stirred the concoction for a long time – until it became apparent to all of us that no amount of stirring was going to dissolve the powder, at which time he withdrew his finger and, holding the jar between his face and the sun, studied the mixture until the powder had settled and the water was reasonably clear.

Then he invited me to have a sniff.

I put my nose almost into the jar and sniffed. Nothing. No aroma whatsoever, pleasant or otherwise. I sniffed again. Nothing.

I looked first to Ralphie, then to Willie, for an explanation. Willie grinned knowingly, sagely, the grin saying, I know something you don't know, dummy. Then he invited my little brother to have a sniff.

Johnny sniffed several times before declaring that the contents of the jar didn't smell like anything.

Now Ralphie as well as Willie was grinning knowingly. *We know something you don't know, dummies.* When the grinning had done its service, Willie reached into a pocket on the bib of his overalls and withdrew a small bottle that he uncapped and, holding it above the jelly jar, permitted several drops of yellow liquid to fall into the mix of powdered limestone and lemon. Ralphie meanwhile resumed his stirring. Soon enough the small bottle had been recapped and returned to its place in Willie's pocket, and soon enough I was invited again to have a sniff.

Ah, but this time the contents of the jelly jar exuded an aroma that faintly suggested lilacs, and I'm sure that I, too, was grinning when I had had my fill. The formula worked!

I looked at my brother, who, though not my twin, must have been able to decipher what I was thinking. He was grinning like a gopher.

Well, my little brother said, speaking for both of us, I'll be damned!

And both of us were – damned, that is – because the liquid that Willie had dropped into the jelly jar was eau d'lilac stolen from the twins' mother's bedroom. We had therefore been taught how to manufacture perfume; you do it by using, as the operative ingredient, perfume.

Our solace, as it turned out, lay in the aromas and the vistas provided by the haymow, where from time to time, before winter set in, my brother and I went to dangle our legs from the open door until the swallows swooped and dipped, announcing dusk, and we would retreat then back into the hay, the loose and the baled, there to inhale those scents we had enjoyed before our sister tattled – except that now the aromas seemed somehow heightened, hay and stillness mingling with those traces of milk and mash and manure rising from those stanchions where the cows had stood slobbering grain as the milkers with their seductive rhythms sucked the rich milk from their udders. Not far from where we sat picking our teeth with a hay straw rested many buckets of rocks, none of them very likely to be spent, because for the moment my brother and I had lost our lust for blood. And it was this loss, I believe, that heightened our senses, that made our breathing sweeter and our viewing clearer, more distinct. We would wait until the mow had filled with swallows, wait until they had settled into their night, then we would return to the door and to the dangling of our feet, and there we would sit looking at the stars and maybe counting a few of them, maybe locating the Big Dipper or the Pleiades, and I would think of the Kiowa and his story of the seven sisters, how they escaped from their brother who had become a bear, how they had thus traded one brief life for an immortal one, how they must be happy up there too high ever to be reached, happy up there making me and my brother happy down here, and time would pass too quickly, gone in the twinkling of an eye, and my brother and I knew that before long we would hear what we dreaded to hear, but neither of us would speak of it, it being the only off note in an otherwise utopian composition – our mother's voice calling us in.

6

HAD WE STAYED on the ranch more than eleven months, I probably would not have learned the following:

Hitler has only got one ball.
Goering has two, but very small.
Himmler has something similar,
But poor old Goebbels has no balls at all.

We improvised individual tunes, though later I'd learn that "Colonel Bogie" was the official tune, and we sang the song with gusto, not only because it was naughty but because its naughtiness was justified: Those square-headed Germans with their square-headed helmets and their square-headed lexicon – Axis, Gestapo, Third Reich – were about to receive their own square-headed comeuppance.

We had returned to the city because the ranch offered a challenge that we could not meet. Father, not experienced as a rancher, was not in the best of health, thanks to (1) a floating kidney, (2) a double hernia, and (3) a right hand that, because of two missing fingers, functioned less than one hundred percent. And the hired hand, a young man whose last name was Ogden, was more interested in alcohol and young women than in milk and bovines. And my brother and I, though we did more or less what we could – carried water to a penned-up bull, pushed loose hay down through a hole in the haymow floor, rode ponies to round up milk cows that needed very little, if any, rounding up – were not big enough to offer any serious assistance. And finally, I believe that my mother was homesick for company, and she had a skill that amounted to talent for making her wishes come true.

So we returned to town.

Jobs. That's what we needed, all of us, to keep our heads, as Mother put it, above water. Mother, willing to set an example and eager to rub shoulders with something more convivial than a milk cow, was hired on as a cook at the local cafe; Father found work with the county as both a utility man and a specialist, his specialty that of driving a road grader on a multiplicity of gravel roads, his expertise most in demand following rain showers; my sister was on call as a house cleaner; my little brother served as an apprentice to his older brother, who became a mower of lawns and a paperboy.

As a mower of lawns the older brother found himself blessed in more ways than one. True, the work itself was not altogether a pleasure, because south central Kansas was where the world's most expansive area of buffalo grass roamed, and buffalo grass, if permitted to grow more than one inch above the ground, was pretty much impossible to cut, unless one attacked it with a machete. Then, too, the older brother's mower, a hand-me-down, was difficult to push; the blades slipped frequently out of adjustment, and on those rare occasions when they were properly adjusted they were not very sharp. So the older brother did not *mow* the grass as much as he *worried* or *pestered* it into a temporary submission.

Worry was my mother's middle name. She worried that the roof of the hand-dug cave would collapse and smother her two sons to death. She worried that her children would not receive a sufficient education in the small country school they attended while living on the ranch. She worried that her children might go cold in the winter and shoeless in the summer. She worried that the next meal might not be forthcoming. At the same time, she did not disparage the act of worrying; she in fact believed, I believe, that to worry is to take the first step in the direction of solving the problem, curing the ill, delaying, if not avoiding, the disaster. She seemed to feel that worry and faith were first cousins, that each, in its own inimitable way, could move mountains.

Because I am my mother's older son I, too, believe in the power of extreme concern, a belief that I shared with my mower; together we worried the buffalo grass until, behold, the lawn lay short-clipped, its pesky buffalo blades more or less even. Finishing the job, then, and looking upon it and pronouncing it good was one of the blessings that derived from the mowing of lawns. Another, of course, was the money – which wasn't much but which covered most of the necessities – the latest issue of the *Torch and Toro*, say, and a malt now and then and a game or two of pool.

And, several times a week, a movie – several times, and sometimes every night because Earl W. Shutt, who owned and operated the Rialto, gave me seven free passes each time I mowed his lawn. Sweet Jesus! Seven free passes! And it was up to me to keep a record of the mowings, dates and hours and such, as well as the number of free passes I had accumulated. Believe this much: I mowed Earl W. Shutt's lawn with catholic regularity. Earl W. Shutt's buffalo grass was worried into submission two or three times a week so that by the end of the mowing season I would have earned enough free passes to see me through the winter and at least halfway into spring.

Add to this boondoggle a second job, that of delivering papers, which though not a boondoggle was nonetheless a way to earn additional money, and an education. I began with a morning route; the *Hutchinson Herald* was the paper, and each morning at an indecent hour I'd find a bundle of these papers lying on the sidewalk near the door to Urie's barber shop. I would sit on the cement and fold them, then deliver them, and more often than not I'd return to the barber shop to find it open and filled with bewhiskered men and the divine reek of sweet pea talcum and bay rum. I enjoyed listening to the banter of men who blew more smoke than they did fire, men who with words kicked various and sundry asses up somewhere between their various and sundry shoulder blades, men who knew, because they said so, shit from Shinola, men who were new at farming and men who had long retired from the drudgery of farming, or threatened to, men who laughed often and easily and loudly, who owned businesses that were doing pretty well, all things considered, or not so well, who knew how to conduct a war and how not to, who needed a shave or a haircut, or both, or didn't but wanted to hang out with those who did, men who for an assortment of reasons left their beds at first light to find their way to Urie's barber shop, where Urie, all five feet of him, stood waiting to serve them.

In Urie's shop is where I first saw a copy of the *Sporting News*, J. G. Taylor Spink, editor and publisher. Its size was that of a tabloid, easily an inch thick, and it contained more baseball information than a boy could assimilate in a lifetime. J. G. Taylor Spink. Such a goofy name, yet, I thought, he must be wealthy beyond measurement. And he must know more about the national pastime than anyone – with the possible exception of Urie, who worshiped first the National League and next its favorite offspring, the Brooklyn Dodgers. In the beginning, Urie would say, God created the National League. And he looked upon it and saw that it was good. So he created the Brooklyn Dodgers, and seeing that they were likewise good, as an organization, he created individuals to comprise the team, among them a centerfielder, Pistol Pete Reiser, who, because he refused to acknowledge the existence of walls, suffered many concussions – seventy times seven, Urie said – but he kept right on playing.

Urie says all of this, or words to this effect, while he is working on a customer – a retired farmer, say, who lying under Urie's razor, his brown face half smooth, half lathered, has drifted into a half-sleep, his serenity a flesh-and-blood definition of faith. Before Urie finishes with him, before he rises from the chair to reach for his wallet to make things right, Urie will have covered the Dodgers from the playing field to the bullpen, and in the process will have taken two or three short breaks, between players, between innings, to go to the back room to steady his hand.

I remember someone saying that Urie's commitment to the Dodgers amounted to a form of idolatry, and I thought of this one morning as I sat on the green bench, the *Sporting News* on my lap, watching and listening to Urie talk about his National Leaguers, his words paying homage, or so someone said, to a graven image. And I wondered if my Sunday school teacher might have had Urie, or his like, in mind when she told her class about the awful dangers inherent in the worshiping of false idols. She said that God said that He would have no other gods before Him, and that included graven images – a figure made of stone, say, or a calf made of gold, something lavish and expensive – but it included also the more mundane object, such as the comic book or the pocket knife, anything, however large or small, expensive or comparatively cheap, that one pays undue attention to. And because I spent a lot of time reading comic books and whittling, I thought she might be speaking to me. But I was there in Sunday school, wasn't I, listening to my teacher, so surely my reading of comic books and my fondness for Barlows did not amount to idolatry, at least not yet.

But Urie, I knew, did not listen to any Sunday school teacher, because he didn't attend church; instead, he spent most of his Sundays fishing, and maybe that was another type of idolatry – because when he wasn't talking about the Brooklyn Dodgers he was talking about the fish he had caught most recently or about the one he was about to catch on Sunday.

To make certain that her students understood the wages of idolatry my Sunday school teacher more than once recounted the story of Shadrach, Meshach, and Abednego, three names that rolled melodically off her tongue. She was an elderly woman who had been teaching Sunday school at the United Brethren church since long before I was born, and she knew her Bible, she said, like the back of her hand, which by now was covered impressively with dark brown spots, which later I'd learn have some complex relationship to the liver. Shad-rach, she'd say, Me-shach, she'd say, and then Abed-ne-go, she'd say, so precisely and so lyrically they might have been her own children. You listened to the words as she pronounced them and you wanted to set them to music, as somebody by now surely has. And Nebuchadnezzar, that egoistic king of Babylon who made a golden image sixty cubits high and six cubits wide – she said that name, too, without stumbling, and she told, *recited*, the story, without a hitch, the names of the four principals serving as a refrain, how the king not only constructed the image, whatever it was, but having constructed it demanded that all of the rulers in all of the adjoining provinces, from the governors and captains and counselors to the judges and the sheriffs, fall down and worship it, their cue being the sound produced by a band comprised of a cornet, a flute, a harp, a sackbut, a psaltery, and a dulcimer.

And what if they refused? Well, then they would be thrown into a fiery furnace and consumed by its flames.

The king's subalterns, not wanting to be consumed by the flames in the fiery furnace, fell down before the golden image when they heard the music from the cornet, flute, harp, sackbut, psaltery, and dulcimer, and some of them said, O king, live on forever!

However, three men refused to worship the king by way of worshiping the golden image – and they were Shadrach, Meshach, and Abednego, who insisted that should they be tossed into the fiery furnace their God would deliver them. The king of course did not believe them, and to make certain that the flames did their work he had the heat increased seven times, whereupon the three dissenters were thrown into the furnace where, behold, they were indeed not consumed by the white-hot flames; they were instead protected by a form that, according to our Sunday school teacher, was a likeness of the Son of God.

So impressed was Nebuchadnezzar the king that on the spot he converted to the god who had protected Shadrach, Meshach, and Abednego – not only converted, but decreed that anyone who spoke amiss against the god of Shadrach, Meshach, and Abednego would be cut into pieces and their houses turned into dunghills, after which he gave Shadrach and Meshach and Abednego promotions, though he didn't say exactly what the promotions entailed.

It has taken me a long time to realize the extent to which the story, any story, relies upon a melody, however subtle that melody might be. Listening to my Sunday school teacher recite the story of Shadrach, Meshach, and Abednego, I was awed not only by the savage pride of Nebuchadnezzar and the spineless subservience of his many subalterns – folks who permitted themselves to be herded like the sheep they apparently were – but I was moved by my teacher's voice, its music, its lilt, its cadences, its lyrical conviction, all of these provoked and guided by names and repetitions fraught with music.

The composition began with the music of individual names – Shadrach, Meshach, and Abednego, certainly, but also the names of instruments – cornet, flute, harp, sackbut, psaltery, dulcimer – names that, repeated, provided a refrain. Add to all of this the titles, the governors and the captains and the counselors and so forth, and what you have are lyrics by way of litanies. Add to this my teacher's voice speaking each word as if she both understood and approved it, and that included *cubit*, *sackbut*, *psaltery*, and *dunghill* – they tripped off her tongue without apology or hesitation, making it apparent that she delighted in and approved of Nebuchadnezzar's trading one brand of fanaticism for another.

And it occurs to me now that perhaps all writing aspires to be music, but too often the words get in the way – tired words and inflated words, words vague and unduly ambiguous, words that exclude and incite, words that encourage the narrow, the shallow, the vindictive. Black Elk, a Native American who had a vision that he blamed himself for being unable to interpret, said that all things aspire to roundness, and perhaps *all things* means what it says, *all things*, the abstract as well as the specific. The concept is summarized clearly and cleanly by Black Elk in John Neihardt's *Black Elk Speaks*:

Everything the Power of the World does is done in a circle. The sky is round, and I have heard that the earth is round like a ball, and so are all the stars. The wind, in its greatest power, whirls. Birds make their nests in circles, for theirs is the same religion as ours. The sun comes forth and goes down again in a circle. The moon does the same, and both are round. Even the seasons form a great circle in their changing, and always come back again to where they were. The life of a man is a circle from childhood to childhood, and so it is in everything where power moves. Our tepees were round like the nests of birds, and these were always set in a circle, the nation's hoop, a nest of many nests, where the Great Spirit meant for us to hatch our children.

Ah, roundness. Ah, music, that consummation all writing aspires to. And perhaps the spoken word wants to be music, too, music that in its own form of roundness returns again and again, as does the sun, to warm and to enlighten. If so, then surely Black Elk was a virtuoso and his friend John Neihardt, a blue-chip accompanist.

Urie the barber, as I viewed him, was not a fanatic, perhaps because he didn't have the power to force his preferences on everyone else. He loved the Dodgers, yes, and he would rather go fishing than accompany his wife to church. But he was, after all, only a barber, not a king; by moving a handle at the side of his chair this way and that he could lower or elevate his customer, but that was pretty much the extent of his power. In his own ways he worshiped baseball and the baited hook – and not infrequently the bottle – but he did not resort to bribery or threats or hocus-pocus to enlist disciples.

So maybe my own preoccupation with comic books and pocket knives fell short of idolatry. I hope so. Neither would last very long, I believe, in a fiery furnace, and I would not have gone into the furnace without them.

My favorite comic characters were the Torch and Toro, though Wonder Woman, Captain Marvel, Batman, Superman, and a dozen others were not far behind. Consider this: a fresh copy of the *Torch and Toro* in your hands as you sit on the green bench in Urie's barber shop on a Saturday afternoon, reading, or pretending to, as you watch Urie shave a man's Adam's apple as he bemoans Pistol Pete's current batting average. The shop is rife with clippings and tonic, tobacco and lather, and warm June air that a white fan not much larger than a dime is trying to circulate. You have long since delivered copies of the *Hutchinson Herald* to your customers, all of them eager to read about the goings-on in Europe. Because the Allied forces have landed and all hell, they say, has broken loose. But at the moment it's the good angels, not the Lucifers, who seem to be winning. The crossing of the English Channel earlier this month was what one writer called "the greatest military gamble in history," and the men in Urie's barber shop agree with General Eisenhower: We will accept nothing less than full victory.

Meanwhile, Virgil Schmidt, who owns the hatchery and who darkens the door of my church only once a year, on Easter Sunday, to stand in the foyer to give each child a newborn chick that the child will have loved to death before nightfall, predicts that the World Series this year will feature the Cardinals and the Browns. Cloyd Stocker, by way of disagreeing, says, Bullshit.

It is not possible for Urie always to control or dominate the conversation, nor do I believe that he wants to. He would talk indefinitely about the Dodgers, yes, or about the prospects of hooking a bigmouth this weekend at the Anthony lake, but when the dialogue strays into lesser pastures – the war, the Series, the most recent local scandal – Urie yields graciously; at such times he listens with a bemused smile as he tends to his snipping and shaving. Urie has very bad teeth, which gives his bemused smile a slight but savage edge.

Stocker says he saw in the paper that a one-armed outfielder playing for a team he can't remember the name of whacked a home run – three hundred and thirty feet, he thinks it was, and over a fence twenty feet high. Virgil Schmidt says, Bullshit.

Now I remember, Stocker says. The Memphis Chicks. The outfielder's right arm was cut off close to the shoulder.

That makes him a southpaw, then, doesn't it, Virgil says, whether he likes it or not.

Well, says Leland Bonham, who farms a half section of red dirt south of town, between Attica and Hazelton, here's another one. The Red Sox just signed a prep-school hotdog for three hundred fifty dollars a month plus a fifteen thousand dollar bonus.

I read that story, too, says a man I don't know. But he'll never make the grade. He has a bad leg, has to wear a brace. Navy gave the sumbitch a medical discharge. Can earn a goddam fortune playing baseball but the sumbitch can't fight for his country.

Now I remember, says Stocker. Name's Pete Gray. But I can't remember the name of the team he was up against.

Bullshit, Virgil says, but not necessarily in response to Stocker; he delivers the word in a tone that suggests an overall assessment.

Can you imagine getting paid three hundred and fifty dollars a month for playing catch with a baseball? asks Bonham.

He can play baseball but the sumbitch can't fight for his country, says the stranger.

Urie douses his customer with bay rum, slicks down his hair with a comb, then whitens his neck with sweet pea talcum. I am turning the pages of the *Torch and Toro*, glancing at them from time to time to see balls of fire finding their scurrilous victims. In an instant the Torch and Toro can flame up, can turn themselves into crime fighting infernos, their weapons balls of fire the duo can manipulate with unerring accuracy.

Now I remember, Stocker says. It was the Chattanooga Lookouts. From Chattanooga.

It is a Saturday afternoon in late June 1944, and in Europe all hell, they say, has broken loose. The war, according to the *Hutchinson Herald*, is proceeding on three fronts, and I will be a First Lieutenant in the United States Marine Corps, First Division, Seventh Regiment, Third Battalion, Weapons Company, Anti-Tank Assault Platoon, before I begin to understand what the hell "three fronts" means. Nor can I grasp the far-off whereabouts of the Allied troops – Cherbourg, Rouen, Dunkirk, Dieppe. But I read about them, and I listen to what others say about them, about the movements of the troops and their sometimes melodic locations, and I put it all together, or try to, and conclude that we, the Allies, the Allied Command, are winning.

Urie handles the strop like the professional he is, flipping it over from its coarse to its fine side so deftly, so quickly, that it makes a sound like *strop*. It is the sound I imagined the strop made that day my buddy R. D. took a beating from his father for engaging in a BB gun war. Urie meanwhile works the razor up and down the leather band until somehow he must know that the edge of the blade is ready. A new customer sits in the chair rubbing his whiskers, waiting.

Stocker says he read that more than four thousand Allied ships crossed the channel on the first day, not counting the small boats.

Eisenhower knows what he's doing, Virgil Schmidt says. Didn't he grow up in Kansas?

I sit on the green bench, watching, listening, not much looking at the *Torch and Toro*. I try to imagine four thousand ships. I try to imagine one. It looks like a picture I saw on the front page of yesterday's *Hutchinson Herald*. Four thousand. Four thousand ships. And each of them carrying – how many? And how many of these were killed or wounded at Omaha Beach? And at other beaches? And in six weeks the German losses, they'll say, will have reached more than two hundred and eighty thousand, not including the fatalities at a place called Minsk. Jesus.

Urie, speaking to the man he's about to shave, the stranger, tells him that Pete Reiser was only twenty-two when he won the National League batting crown. Three forty-three, Urie says. He hit three forty-three. That was in 1941, the same year we got into the war.

What I don't understand, Stocker says, is why didn't the goddam Luftwaffe bomb any of the ships while they were crossing the Channel.

Eisenhower knows what he's doing, Virgil says.

Germans, Stocker says. They don't know shit from Shinola. We'll have their asses kicked up between their shoulder blades before the end of the year.

Victory. V is for victory. Dot-dot-dot-dash. There's a German in the grass with a bullet up his you-know-what. Push it in, pull it out, Uncle Sam, Uncle Sam. Victory. The word in the mouth makes the mouth water. The thrill of impending victory is sweet to the taste, and infectious.

Here's the problem: Our town is about to be attacked by a battalion, maybe a regiment, more likely a division, of Krautheads masquerading as common sparrows. They are expected to make their move tonight shortly after dusk, after they have rendezvoused at an

83

assembly point somewhere south of the railroad tracks between the grain elevator and the train station. If they are not met with powerful resistance they can be expected to cause heavy damage to the town, and perhaps wipe it out entirely.

Here's the solution: surprise the enemy force with sufficient firepower to inflict enough casualties to cause it to retreat and to do this with a flanking movement calculated to permit no routes of escape.

Both the problem and the solution are posed by General Jack Giggy, who owns the BB gun that almost a year ago I borrowed for the shootout with my buddy. R. D. Giggy is three years older than I, and he knows pretty much everything – who the enemy is, for example, and what the enemy intends to do, and where to obtain BBs for his air rifle. He has given me the rank of sergeant, and my brother the rank of corporal.

I locate my favorite slingshot, and walking the back roads I find more than enough ammunition. My brother, too, fills his pockets with rocks, though his assignment is not to wield a slingshot but instead to carry the flashlight that, as on the ranch, he will use to mystify the Krauts.

General Giggy knows almost everything because he lives with his grandparents and they trust him to do whatever he pleases because he would do whatever he pleases, anyway. But though independent, the general is also reliable, good-humored, imaginative. He suffers from asthma; always his breathing is labored, and the rasp in his voice suggests a maturity beyond its years. He enjoys telling stories, most of them deriving from experiences beyond the city limits of Attica. General Giggy, on impulse, will hitchhike to a nearby town – Sharon, for example, with its tavern and its high percentage of Catholics – and then, having hitchhiked home, will tell stories of beer drinkers and dancers and sometimes fist fighters, my brother and I held spellbound by his animated re-enactments. He never speaks of his parents – or of his elderly grandparents, for that matter. They seem to have an inveterate faith that Jack is at heart a good boy and will never disappoint or betray them.

Shortly after sundown my brother and I are standing where we were told to be, on the loading dock at the depot. The front pockets of my overalls are obese with rocks. So, too, the front pockets of Corporal Johnny's overalls, though the corporal will not have a flashlight until General Giggy arrives. My slingshot is in a hip pocket itching to bring down a Kraut.

The depot, a mustard yellow structure, is at the south edge of town where the main line of the Panhandle Division of the Atchison, Topeka, and Santa Fe stretches east to Harper and south, after a long and lazy curve, to Alva, Oklahoma. Freights and passenger trains keep the rails shiny as new dimes; you can stand on the loading dock and feel their awful weight as they rumble one direction or the other, and sometimes they come to a slow, deliberate, labored stop, their engines gurgling and hissing, to drop off a passenger, or to let one on, or to take on water.

This evening as we await the arrival of Giggy we can stand at the east edge of the dock and looking north see the main street all the way almost to the high school. It is Saturday, the final Saturday in the month, and some of the businesses, we know, will not close until well after midnight – Moulton's grocery, for example, will probably still be open after the pool hall and the drugstore have closed. Because another harvest is about to end, trucks and pickups of all descriptions stretch in line from the elevator just across the narrow macadam highway up the main street to where the highway doglegs west, a line that will crawl its way to the elevator for several hours after dusk has turned to darkness.

It's a clear night and of course the smell of wheatgrain is in the air, and so too the sounds of a vibrant small-town economy – the idlings of the trucks, the groanings of those same trucks as one by one they take their places on the scales to be weighed before dumping their loads. And the whir of the augers as they lift the grain into one of the elevator's spacious bins.

Giggy arrives with a three-cell flashlight in one hand and his BB gun in the other. The rasp in his voice more pronounced than I have ever heard it, he gives us a final briefing. See that cottonwood over there between us and the elevator? Yes, we see it. We have seen it many times. It is the largest cottonwood in town, its highest limb reaching only a few feet short of the Seven Sisters, its trunk massive, its leaves like the stars not countable. See that elevator over there? Yes, we see it. We have been looking at it for more than a few minutes, watching trucks and pickups spill their grain into it in the light of its many bulbs. Well, says the general, the Krauts will soon be at their initial rendezvous station at the elevator, after which they will assemble in the cottonwood before they attack our town.

I nod. The corporal, having taken the flashlight from the general, nods. Need anything more be said?

And when the sparrows arrive they arrive in droves so thick that I believe all three of us are genuinely surprised. They settle on the ground near the elevator, there to gorge themselves on grain that has spilled from overloaded vehicles, grain that over the past two weeks has gathered and scattered and gathered again, providing a vast and ongoing banquet for the sparrows, a feast to end all feasts – until maybe, the Lord and the rainfall willing, next year.

Sated, the sparrows will fly into the cottonwood, drove by drove, until all of them have disappeared.

At which time we will make our move. Giggy with his BB gun will take the lead, the sergeant and the corporal not far behind. We will move to what the general calls the tree's starboard flank, though it is difficult to know exactly where starboard is, the tree being round. Giggy, however, seems to know what his subalterns don't so that when he stops and instructs the corporal to work the light, we know that we are standing at the starboard flank.

The beam from the three-cell flashlight is strong and bright, but the Krauts, though German, seem to have learned the distinction between shit and Shinola; they have hidden themselves among the leaves and the limbs of the cottonwood so skillfully that only occasionally do we catch a glimpse of what looks to be feathers. When we catch a glimpse we open fire, BBs and rocks switching the leaves, at times hitting a limb to *ric-o-chet* into more leaves and limbs, until

I empty first one pocket, then another, then after a short break dip into the corporal's reserves.

I do not know what brought down the sparrow, BB or rock. But the bird fell dead onto the bare ground beneath the cottonwood, and when the general kicked it softly to see if it were truly dead and it was obvious that it was, he smiled, and I smiled, too, and the corporal smiled, and we left the body where it was and went uptown to see what was going on.

7

IN THE POOL HALL both pool and snooker tables are occupied and so too the domino tables. Butch Mischler, owner and operator, shuffles from one game to another, racking balls, collecting money from the losers, and leaving chips in the form of small rectangular pieces of thin orange cardboard for the winners. On each side of the chip are the words *Attica Recreation Parlor*. Each chip is worth a nickel. Collect enough chips and you can redeem them for pop, candy, or – when Butch's allotment of cigarettes comes in, if it does – a package of Camels or Lucky Strikes.

I feel at home in the pool hall, in the *rec-re-a-tion par-lor*, partly because Butch is a friendly man who knows how harmless I am, partly because at age eleven I can hold my own with a cue stick, and partly because there is no liquor sold on the premises (my town is a dry town), meaning that Butch's venue is not a very likely candidate for any type of shootout where a young boy might find himself caught in a crossfire.

The place is sweetly thick with cigarette smoke. I inhale deeply, exhale slowly, pretending that the air is the Chesterfield I'm holding in my rough, yellowed fingers. I walk to the southeast corner of the parlor where painted plywood and a blue blanket for a door define the men's room.

I would love to be old enough to buy cigarettes for myself, old enough to tap one from its tight, lovely package and light it with a wooden match similar to the ones that I so innocently ignited our kitchen with. Once in a while I'll come into one of these beautiful objects by chance, when Giggy gives me one, for example, one that he has lifted from God knows where, or when by chance I spot my father's package of Camels lying somewhere unguarded and I fail to resist temptation; but most of the time I am reduced to the inhaling of other people's smoke, or to improvisation.

In the old days, before I began mowing lawns, before I earned my way into the Rialto by trimming Earl W. Shutt's buffalo grass with the dull blades of my pusher mower, I went to the movies by resting my back against the outside wall at the rear of the Rialto; not far behind me, then, and inside, was the movie screen. In front of me, say about thirty feet, was the alley that ran from beyond Moulton's grocery store to the north to another grocery store, this one little more than a hole in the wall, to the south. Beside me, his back also against the wall, my buddy R. D.

We, of course, had planned our strategy carefully: He would bring the toilet paper and the matches, and I would bring the coffee.

Coffee is one of several staples I could count on; it would not be difficult to find an empty Prince Albert can and fill it with Folgers from our kitchen. And R. D. apparently had no trouble securing from his own cupboards a small pallet of toilet paper and a fistful of Diamond matches.

Here is the scene: a warm night in July or August, no clouds, maybe a slight breeze coming down the alley from the south. Two young boys in overalls kneeling behind the picture show, their fingers improvising cigarettes. If the night is in early July, say the end of the first week, an aroma of sulfur and potassium nitrate will be hanging like a thin invisible coverlet of gauze in the darkening air. On their knees, the boys will roll some coffee into a square of tissue, will lick the tissue then to secure the coffee, will lay the finished tube aside to make way for the improvising of another.

Oh shit, R. D. might say, or, Sweet Jesus!

So tell us this, Sister Hook: How beautiful, when all is said and done, might heaven be?

It might indeed be beautiful, supremely and majestically and ultimately beautiful – if the night is balmy and clear and a new Roy Rogers movie is playing at the Rialto and you are in cahoots with a buddy whose expertise in the field of the improvised cigarette is equal almost to yours.

By the time the cartoons have ended we have a pyramid of lovely white tubes sufficient unto our aspirations. Pyramid between us, we lean back against the wall to absorb the movie with our spines and ears as we absorb the smoke from our improvisation with our lungs.

It is important to understand that sometimes a little bit goes a long way. We know, for example, because we have been here before, that to inhale deeply is to invite a coughing spell of serious proportions – so, having nursed the coffee to life with kitchen matches we inhale briefly and gingerly, then take our time, and much of it, exhaling. For we have spent a lot of our lives watching others smoke, and we have learned that much of the pleasure derives from mannerisms – the way one uses his fingers to manipulate the cigarette, the extent to which one permits the ashes to accumulate before one flicks them down and away, the art involved in the holding of the cigarette between one's lips, moving it from one edge of the mouth to the other with the tip of the tongue, without inhaling, and certainly the nonchalance with which one handles, or fails to handle, that portion of the smoke that finds its way into one's eyes.

Behind us the plot of the movie unfolds by way only of words and music, yet we have no trouble whatsoever delineating the good guys from the bad, the high moments from the low. The tones of voice, together with the words, tell us whether to listen carefully or light up another Folgers cigarette, and the music tells us the rest. Because we know that eventually the badasses, as R. D. calls them, will be knocked off their horses and pummeled into red dust somewhere in no-man's-land, we do not concern ourselves with the question of ultimate justice; we will listen intently, when the time comes, to the final chase, to the thundering hoofbeats, to the music that builds to an almost deafening crescendo, and to the quaint sounds that the fist makes when it strikes the human face.

Meanwhile, we lean back and strike matches and put their flames to the toilet tissue and the Folgers coffee. We do not always finish one cigarette before we light another, and perhaps the mannerisms at times outnumber, and thus outlast, the inhalations. Yes, heaven is behind the picture show as well as somewhere among the stars, though the stars, maybe because their distance makes them a type of forbidden fruit, have their undeniable appeal, too.

When Roy begins to sing, then to yodel, we know that it's time to bury what remains of the evidence and light out for home. And when we reach the gravel road that separates R. D.'s house from mine, I offer him what I know he needs: a fresh stick of Juicy Fruit gum.

I use the toilet, stand reading the message above the urinal for perhaps the hundredth time – *Stand up close, the next person might be barefooted* – then I leave the pool hall to investigate the goings-on in the drugstore. The line of trucks in the main street appears as long as ever; I look north to see it extending, as it had when I stood on the loading dock at the depot, beyond the dogleg where the highway turns west.

What happens next is something I can't yet altogether account for, except to guess that Myron Bateman was (1) drunk or (2) wanting to be drunk because before I could enter the drugstore he called to me from his loaded grain truck. And I hesitated because I thought he might have taken me for someone else, but when he called again I could hear my name plainly, so I walked over to the truck.

Myron was out of the cab by the time I reached him. I knew him reasonably well. He attended my church, the United Brethren. I was pretty sure he wasn't drunk, though I knew next to nothing about how a drunk man might look, or talk. But I was pretty sure he was okay.

Get up there in the cab, Myron said. If you'd like to earn a quarter or two.

I was onto the running board and into the cab, behind the wheel, almost before I knew what I was doing.

You're big enough to handle this rig for a few minutes, aren't you, Myron said.

It was a statement, not a question.

Sure, I said. Hell yes. I'm big for my size.

Good, said Myron. Grandma, that's the slowest gear, is far to the right and up. Just keep her moving as the line moves. You won't even have to use the footfeed.

And he slammed the door shut and disappeared into the drugstore.

And suddenly, though I was indeed big for my size, I felt infinitely small; in the twinkling of an eye I went from warrior-who-brings-down-Krauthead to boy-who-doesn't-know-shit from-Shinola.

But I was in no position either to whine or look for excuses. I was behind the wheel of a truck almost as large as my grandfather's farmhouse, a truck whose bed was overflowing with grain, and my choice was flat simple: fish or cut bait.

I fished – that is, I found the clutch with my left foot, the brake with my right, and when the time came to move forward, I found Grandma. And of course Mr. Bateman had been correct: I didn't need to use the footfeed. Instead, I released the clutch slowly, and my truck responded, a low growl in her mighty throat as she crept heavily and inexorably forward.

In only a few minutes I had mastered the ritual of the start and the stop, and in only a few minutes more my apprehension had turned into a confidence that bordered on the downright cocky. Find Grandma. Release the clutch, slowly. Stop when the red eyes of the truck ahead light up my hood. Return the gear stick to neutral.

Then wait, and wait, and do some watching through a rolled-down window, or maybe do some thinking, until the truck in front of you again moves forward. And you have plenty of time, you tell yourself, because the elevator is yet a good two blocks away, Moulton's grocery store at your right, Skeet Lew's five-and-dime to the south beside it, followed in turn by the post office, the Rialto, Trent's shoe repair, Trotter's hole-in-the-wall grocery, the Champlin service station, then finally the depot, east of which, across the highway, is the off road that leads to the elevator. You are moving slowly, in short, easy increments. You have plenty of time.

But Mr. Bateman doesn't return, and you are now even with the Rialto, where *Coney Island* starring Betty Grable is on the marquee, so your thick wall of confidence begins to erode. You worry first that Mr. Bateman will not return, that you will be forced to drive his mighty truck with its load of golden grain all the way to where the off road leads to the elevator, to the scales that will weigh both the truck and its cargo before the dumping, then after you have circled back will weigh the truck without its load, and. . . . Jesus. You think that maybe your skills as a truck driver do not extend far enough to cover such an exigency, and you find yourself driving with your head out of the window, looking for any sign whatsoever of Mr. Bateman.

You worry also that Mr. Bateman, when he appears, will be so drunk that he will not be able to assume the wheel. You don't know much about drunkenness, only that some men who have over-indulged become loud and cantankerous and unsteady on their feet. What if Mr. Bateman shows up in such a condition? He had disappeared into the drugstore, and though your town is a dry town you have heard stories about there being liquor available in the drugstore, under the front counter, perhaps, or more likely somewhere in the back room where prescriptions are filled by the man who no doubt knows where John Barleycorn is hidden.

I was first introduced to John Barleycorn by my fourth grade teacher, Miss Vermilia, who one morning after the Pledge of Allegiance told us not to bother just now with our arithmetic; she had a special treat for us, and she wanted us to sit quietly with our desks uncluttered and watch and listen carefully. Then with a new piece of chalk she wrote this word on the blackboard: CRUSADER. She spent a few minutes then explaining the word, and with it its first cousin, CRUSADE, after which she nodded in the general direction of the hallway and, behold, a short, barrel-chested man with black hair parted precisely down the middle materialized. In his right hand he carried a white shoebox with T-U-B-E in red letters on the sides and the top.

For the next half hour or so this man, who introduced himself as Tubeman, talked about the many insidious dangers, not of alcohol – that would come later, with different personnel – but of tobacco, a substance that I would not come fully to appreciate for a couple of years, after R. D. and I had learned to roll our own with Folgers coffee. Tubeman had a ruddy face and a winning smile; he wore an undersized yellow T-shirt that made his barrel chest impressively muscled, as were his biceps. He first spoke in general terms about tobacco, then, with the help of large black-and-white photographs held by Miss Vermilia, who had taken the pictures from the center drawer of her desk, he moved into specifics, the photos, or most of them, depicting Tubeman during various stages of his life, from early youth to the present. The early photos revealed a boy thin as a rail with a hang-dog face and eyes that seemed to be looking at something, or someone, they had no intention of believing. He had several of these early stage pictures, all of them intended to illustrate this message: When you are young do not indulge tobacco. Tubeman told us how he had become addicted when he was in the fourth grade, this very grade my classmates and I were at this very moment in, and so heavy was the addiction that it led to this: a photo that far eclipsed, in suggesting detachment, agony, and despair, all of the others.

I was thankful, of course, that the middle stage of Tubeman's addiction was not quite so alarmingly graphic. Little by little, thanks be to the God who hates tobacco as much as He loves children, Tubeman began to escape from the shackles that bound him – each phase of the escape illustrated with black-and-white photographs – until at last he emerged absolutely unshackled, a free man now capable of becoming the man he had been created to be. And that man, he said, stands now before you, and you can see with your own eyes what that man has become!

There was then a prolonged and appreciative silence as my peers and I looked closely at what Tubeman had become – both in black-and-white and in person. He was indeed a striking figure, his yellow T-shirt barely able to contain him. During the silence Miss Vermilia held up the photographs that constituted the third and final stage, pictures that revealed Tubeman in an assortment of postures, each of them a sharply focused testimony to his physicality. And I should mention, too, that the far-off, vacuous look that had dominated the early photos had given way to a blue brightness that would have made me think of sea water and sunny beaches had I ever seen them.

When Tubeman broke the silence, Miss Vermilia returned the photos to the middle drawer of her desk and retired to a chair near the west wall, under a high window not far from the blackboard, to become herself a member of the congregation.

Then did Tubeman reach for and display the white shoebox with T-U-B-E on its sides and top. By this time I had connected Tubeman with the word that Miss Vermilia had written on the blackboard: Tubeman was a crusader.

He turned the box this way and that, as if he were a magician wanting to show that no strings were attached to whatever it was he was about to do. Then, deliberately, he removed the lid and just as deliberately he took from the box what looked like a new black rubber inner tube, which in fact it was. Tubeman identified it as such, saying further that the tube would work in any of the tires on his new Studebaker, which was the first new automobile, he said, he had ever owned.

He unfolded the black tube, then gently smoothed out the creases, looking more at the class than at the tube, as if, truth to tell, he could do the entire exercise blindfolded. He then removed a small gadget from a front pocket and with the gadget unscrewed the valve core, telling us along the way what he was doing. When the core came free he placed it gingerly, as if it were a miniscule egg, on Miss Vermilia's desk.

I was enthralled. Here was a crusader standing barrel-chested in front of Miss Vermilia's class, holding a new rubber inner tube, one that, he had said, would work in any of the tires on his new Studebaker, an inner tube with its valve core removed: So what in the name of all that is holy is this crusader going to do?

Just this: inflate the tube with air from his own smoke-free, barrel-chested lungs.

Before taking the stem into his mouth, Tubeman inhaled most of the oxygen in our classroom, his chest becoming roughly the size of a dirigible. Then with a dainty pucker he took the stem into his mouth and with unbelievable force relayed the air from his lungs into the tube, relayed it slowly and doggedly, his face becoming first pink, then red, then something between red and purple, his blue eyes much, much larger than marbles. The tube, it seemed to me, did not want to relent, certainly not at the beginning. But Tubeman was not standing here in Miss Vermilia's classroom to taste defeat; his human willpower against the nonhuman, rubber willpower of the tube would prevail, eventually.

And, behold, it did. The tube grew larger and larger, until at last it both made and belabored Tubeman's point: Stop smoking, and you too will be able to inflate a new black rubber inner tube with the air from your own reconstituted lungs.

When Tubeman had spent himself, he replaced the valve core while permitting only two or three insignificant hisses to escape from the tube. Then, ceremoniously, he pranced to the west side of the room and presented the trophy to our teacher, who accepted it, I thought, with appropriate gratitude and humility. It would be ours to display in our room, at a spot of our choosing, forever.

I was shocked to see, at my right across the sidewalk, Hadsall's Champlin station, Hadsall – standing with his bald head shining under a string of bulbs – holding a hose the end of which disappeared into an anonymous gas tank. Sweet Jesus! Already my truck and I were less than a block from the elevator. Where, oh where, was Mr. Bateman? I was performing the ritual now without thinking: Find Grandma. Release the clutch, slowly. Stop when the red eyes of the truck ahead light up my hood. Return the gear stick to neutral.

And I know something that I'll bet no one else in this long line of burdened vehicles knows – that just ahead, off the highway to the east and under the spreading foliage of the world's largest cottonwood, lies a dead German disguised as a common sparrow, unless a cat or coyote has carried him away. And something else: If that bird were alive and wanting to illustrate the immensity of eternity, it might carry away, one grain at a time, all of the wheat in my truck bed and then all of the wheat in all of the other truck beds, and at the end of all that carrying away less than one second of eternity would have elapsed.

And General Giggy took his BB gun and his flashlight and went home, and my little brother said he was going to the cafe to see his mother and maybe have a hot beef sandwich. And I went into the pool hall to stand close to the urinal to take a leak. And there's a German in the grass with a bullet up his you-know-what. *Push it in, pull it out, Uncle Sam, Uncle Sam.* And I am at one and the same time a man and a nonman, a boy and a nonboy. And when does a boy become a man? John Steinbeck, in his story "Flight," will both pose and answer the question, though I'll not read it for another several years: A boy becomes a man when a man is needed.

At the moment the man most needed is Myron Bateman, who having instructed me in the art of easing a loaded dumptruck forward disappeared into the drugstore, that place I had been headed to when I heard Mr. Bateman call me. Bauman Rexall Drugstore. Chocolate malts and comic books and a pinball machine I sometimes stand beside into the wee awesome hours of the morning. It's the place where my maternal grandmother, Anna Steierl Yock, buys her cough medicine, not realizing, I now am certain, that terpene hydrate laced with codeine can provide a high that might eventually lead to addiction.

And somewhere in the warm and convivial bowels of the drugstore there exists, they say, a cache of strong spirits that perhaps at this moment Mr. Bateman is tapping. Oh, Mr. Bateman, where are you? I find Grandma. I perform the ritual. My truck groans forward. The Champlin station is beginning to fall behind.

The following day Miss Vermilia hit us with the second of her one-two punches. The word CRUSADER had been newly chalked on the blackboard, and I saw it only seconds before I saw two ample women sitting, or trying to, on metal folding chairs at the left of my teacher's desk. They might well have been sisters, even twins, so closely did they resemble each other. They were dressed, or covered, all in black, their dresses reaching their ankles, even as they sat, and their white hair was wound tightly in buns secured by a multitude of short black combs. Their faces were plain, devoid entirely of cosmetics; the word that my mother probably would use is *wholesome*. Wholesome. They were smiling.

Miss Vermilia introduced them as members in good standing of the Women's Christian Temperance Union, an organization I had never heard of. But of course I believed in its existence the moment our teacher spoke its name, because Miss Vermilia, a thin, wiry, kind, no-nonsense disciplinarian, was by no means sympathetic to any form of prevarication. And the ladies are here today, she continued, to talk about and to demonstrate the evils and the dangers of demon rum.

Demon rum. The women in black nodded, as if *demon rum* were a stage cue and they were the leading ladies, as in fact they were. They arose in unison. One assumed a position at the near side of the desk, the other a position at the far side. Miss Vermilia took her seat near the west wall.

The ladies moved eloquently, and without further fanfare, into their production, beginning with a not altogether brief summary of their patron saint, Carry A. Nation, a woman whom they identified as the Hatchet Lady of Medicine Lodge. Did they mean Medicine Lodge, Kansas, that town just twenty-two miles west of our classroom? Yes, they did. Medicine Lodge, Kansas, where Carry A. Nation lived nearly all of her adult life, where the good Hatchet Lady, hatchet in hand, attacked not only those local establishments that sold demon rum illegally, and that included a drugstore or two, but also similar dens of iniquity in Wichita to the east and Kiowa to the south.

At the mention of Carry A. Nation's name Miss Vermilia had arisen from her chair and, walking to her desk, removed a picture of Mrs. Nation from the center drawer. She went then to the blackboard, where she placed the base of the picture on the chalk and eraser tray and tilted the top of the picture against the chalkboard. The woman in the photo strongly resembled the women who were talking about her – except that Mrs. Nation's eyes seemed almost flammable in their intensity, and she was not smiling. Her mouth in a straight line somehow complemented the squarish, bulldog aspect of her countenance. She looked, on balance, more threatening than wholesome.

The WCTU women spoke of Mrs. Nation endearingly, and to be honest I do not know how much of what they said has become entwined with what I much later learned about the woman Robert Lewis Taylor called "America's foremost lady hell-raiser." I do remember that the presentation was superbly timed and polished; one of the ladies might be talking about Mother Nation's personal confrontation with a Medicine Lodge drunk, for example, and having ended a sentence that took the listener to the edge of dialogue, the other lady would assume the role of the drunk and the dialogue would proceed without the slightest hitch. And I remember the extent to which one of the ladies emphasized the divine implications of Mrs. Nation's name. Perhaps they did not mention – or, if they did, downplayed it – that Mother Nation went through a horrendous first marriage before she entered into a second, likewise unfortunate, union, this time with a man whose last name, Nation, would play an important part in the Hatchet Woman's legend.

The woman in black at the east side of the desk went to the blackboard and, careful not to touch the photograph of her subject, took a length of chalk in her right hand and wrote *C. A. N.* in large letters on the board. Then with an eraser she carefully removed the periods. Smiling, as always, she turned to the class and asked what word it was seeing. Almost in harmony the class said, *can*. Yes indeed, said the woman in black, explaining then that CAN was shorthand meaning You CAN do it, Carry! You CAN send old demon rum once and for all to an early grave!

As she spoke these words the other lady, having moved from her station at the west side of Miss Vermilia's desk, took the chalk from her compatriot's hand – the flawless passing of the baton from one runner to another – and across the blackboard wrote *Carry Amelia Nation*. Smiling, she turned to face the class, to give it time to absorb the Hatchet Lady's full and portentous name. Then with an eraser she eliminated *melia* from *Amelia*, leaving the following: *Carry A. Nation*. Again, smiling, she paused to give her audience time to draw whatever conclusions it might be striving to draw. Then, and with obvious pleasure, and for the benefit of those mental laggards among us, she explained that this, too, was God's shorthand, and Mother Nature had transcribed it to be an ultimatum: Carry A. Nation, carry a nation, into sobriety!

And I remember also, I believe, the ladies' account of Mrs. Nation's assault on the saloons in Kiowa, another Kansas town, along with Medicine Lodge, whose name was familiar. The name Medicine Lodge had rung a bell because of an elaborate re-enactment of a peace treaty the city conducted every few years, and I had seen one of these ceremonies only last summer, and its eight-hour-long dramatization had left a deep impression. The re-enactment was held outdoors, two miles east of Medicine Lodge, on a landscape of green valleys that serpentined among and around buttes and hillocks that looked a lot like those in movies of the wild west that in a few years I'd be mowing Earl W. Shutt's lawn for free passes to watch. I didn't understand much of what was going on, but I had been told that it was significant, and I'm sure it was, if not in content then surely in duration. The school bus that delivered us to the site arrived at eight in the morning and departed at four in the afternoon, or was supposed to, and probably would have had not the peace treaty run longer than scheduled. But what I remember most clearly is the contrast between the many Indians that fought in the re-enacted battles and the one Indian on a far-off butte sitting half slumped over on his horse and in his right hand holding what looked to be a long and elaborately decorated spear. And the funny thing is that this Indian with his horse and spear had been standing at the edge of this butte throughout the daylong performance, through all of the bloody battles, men both in uniform and loincloth firing and slashing away at one another, and falling honest-to-

God from honest-to-God horses, and once in a while one of the horses falling, too, and all of the yelping and pointing and loading and reloading and arrows in the air thick as sparrows – through all of this, and more, the Indian sat unmoving bareback half slumped on his horse, until I came to believe that it wasn't an actual person, after all, or an actual horse, but an imitation of some sort, a sculpture, maybe, but when things calmed down and the treaty at last was signed and the red dust in the air began to settle, the Indian raised himself from his slouch and turned his pony and rode slowly away from the edge of the butte and disappeared into one of the landscape's many ravines.

And the name Kiowa rang a bell also, thanks first to the Indian who had told his audience about the mythical creation of the Pleiades, and next to the Kiowa High School cheerleaders, six girls I had seen at a basketball game that R. D. and I attended with our chaperone, General Giggy. During halftime of the game, which our team, the Bulldogs, was winning, six girls dressed scantily in fringed buckskin, their hair in pigtails, performed a dance around a bass drum that had been positioned at the center of the court. Four boys sat cross-legged near the drum, one at each of the four great directions, and several minutes before the girls began their dancing the boys beat a low steady rhythm against the head of the drum: BOOM-boom-boom-boom, BOOM-boom-boom-boom. Then in single file the girls danced lightly onto the court, their moccasins barely touching the glossy hardwood. They were very pretty girls, slim and mobile, their lips bright red, their cheekbones highlighted with small circles of black, the ends of their rubberbanded pigtails bobbing against the bareness of their shoulders and backs. Leaning slightly forward they danced around the drum, two fingers on the left hand raised behind the head to simulate feathers while the right hand beat a delicate rhythm against the mouth, the syncopation of the drum having changed to BOOM-boom-BOOM-boom-BOOM-BOOM-BOOM-BOOM.

Ki-a, ki-a, wah-wah-wah-wah!
Ki-a, ki-a, wah-wah-wah-wah!

We are Chieftains, K-H-S!
And we always do our best!
Ki-a, ki-a, wah-wah-wah-wah!
Ki-a, ki-a, wah-wah-wah-wah!
Ki-a-wah! Ki-a-wah! Chief-tains, FIGHT!

Beside me, my buddy R. D. whispered, with a Pentecostal conviction no doubt inherited from his father, Well, I'll be a son of a bitch!

So when the ladies in black began to talk about Kiowa, about the day that Carry A. Nation assaulted its saloons, I obviously knew something about the hamlet whereof they spoke. They said that Mrs. Nation chose Kiowa because God Himself, in unbroken English, told her to. You must understand, one or the other of the ladies said, that Carry A. Nation often spoke directly with the Almighty and that she never wavered or faltered in her efforts to obey Him. Yes, Lord, she had said that early morning when the Lord singled out Kiowa, Thy will be done – and by midafternoon she was on her way.

She went alone, they said, her favorite horse, Old Prince, pulling a wagon loaded to the gills with rocks, plus a few brickbats and some empty bottles she had scavenged from the roadsides near Medicine Lodge. From Medicine Lodge to Kiowa is a distance of approximately twenty-six miles, all of these traveled, said the women, without so much as a single prolonged stop. Can you imagine? And when she and Old Prince arrived in Kiowa, they went straight to the first of several murder shops, as the lady in black called them. Then, after entering the establishment and shouting, Men! I have come to save you from a drunkard's grave! she proceeded to discharge the rocks and the brickbats and the bottles that she had cradled as if cordwood into the saloon.

As they described the ensuing destruction the ladies in black moved their arms and hands extensively, now lifting a rock or a brickbat or a bottle, now throwing it against an imaginary row of bottles at the back of the classroom while at the same time their facial expressions reflected – in appropriate degrees, I'm guessing –

Mother Nation's anger and heaven-directed determination. Thus did the Hatchet Lady, by way of our ladies in black, make a shambles of our classroom-turned-bar, bottles smashed, chairs splintered, mirrors reduced to shards, children sitting in the center of the mayhem with their mouths open wide enough to catch flies.

One of the several problems of being young is that the older folks often expect us to assimilate and understand, and thereupon react intelligently, to what in our brief but genuine innocence we cannot handle – or don't want to, or would rather, for reasons that we'd prefer not to articulate, postpone. We listen attentively to the two fat women because Miss Vermilia instructed us to listen, and because from her chair in the northwest corner of the room she sits watching us watching the ladies in black, making certain that her instructions are, to a student, being followed.

Not that the ladies in black are not interesting. In many respects they go beyond interesting all the way into ludicrous, and perhaps several leagues beyond; in fervor, animation, and devotion – not to mention bulk – they are sublime. But even as I am fascinated I am confused. I have never in all of my nine years seen a bottle of rum, nor have I ever seen a purported murder shop where the demon is sold. My town is a dry town, and except for occasional under-the-counter medications ostensibly meted out in the Rexall drugstore my town has no up-and-operating saloon.

Even so, listening to the ladies in black as they conclude their demolishing of Dobson's joint in neighboring Kiowa, home of the Chieftains, I find myself both in awe and dread of what I do not understand. And I believe that my classmates are feeling pretty much the same thing, and that the women from the WCTU, sensing our collective awe and fear, determine that the time is ripe for them to shift gears.

Whereupon one of the ladies reaches a hand behind Miss Vermilia's desk and brings forth a large black purse on its way to becoming luggage. Her accomplice then reaches into the bag and withdraws first a one-quart jar half filled with a clear liquid held hostage by a heavy screw-down lid; next she lifts out another jar that precisely, in every detail, resembles the first; and finally, after a long pause, I believe intended further to whet our innocent appetites, she delivers a quart-sized silver tin can that has for a lid a piece of cloth held in place by a rubber band.

As the one lady replaces the purse behind Miss Vermilia's desk, the other lady arranges the receptacles on the desktop, tin can in the center, jars on opposite sides of the can.

Now, say the ladies, pretty much in unison, please watch carefully.

One of them unscrews the lids from the jars while the other removes the cloth from the top of the can. There is another long pause, during which our appetites are further whetted. Then the most curious thing on all of God's green earth transpires: The woman attending the can reaches into it her fleshy fingers and, behold, lifts upward and out of that can the largest night crawler I ever hope to see!

I join my classmates in a gasp. Between her thumb and index finger the night crawler writhes, as if determined to break free and escape to – where? The top of Miss Vermilia's desk? There is of course no place for it to escape to.

Smiling, the captor moves her hand with its victim intact to her right, very slowly, until the crawler finds itself directly above the open mouth of one of the jars, at which point it finds itself released, and it falls wriggling as if an infant eel into the jar's clear liquid.

The other lady meanwhile has dipped her own fleshy fingers into the can and, behold, has lifted up and out another night crawler, its desire not to follow orders on at least a par with its brother. Soon, however, it is swimming in the other jar, and the ritual continues, the crusaders taking turns removing night crawlers from the can to drop them into the jars, until each jar has its equal share of worms.

And now, say the ladies in black, wiping their night-crawler fingers on the unsoiled palms of their other hands, it is time to sing!

And without paying further attention to the crawlers they proceed to teach us the words and the tune to the official Loyal Temperance Legion song, one verse of which I'll herewith share:

Let us tell you, let us tell you,
about the LTL;
we are loyal temperance workers,
and doing mighty well.
We are working, we are working,
for a cause that is just;
come and help us fight this battle,
for win it we must!

They taught us several verses, and a chorus that began *Loyal, faithful, and true, we are a temperance band*, then invited us one by one, by rows, to come forward and examine the contents of the jars. We, of course, looked to Miss Vermilia for approval, and when she nodded and smiled we began the procession, each somewhat embarrassed and self-conscious, yet somehow proud, marching to the desk to view the crawlers at point-blank range. In one of the jars the infant eels were cavorting and swimming as if they had decided to spend their day off at the lake; in the other jar, the night crawlers, their epidermis bleached to a sickly white, were lying in a heap at the bottom of the jar, their bodies no more active than stones. When the viewings were completed, Miss Vermilia herself having paid her respects, the ladies informed us that one of the jars contained water, while the other jar contained – two deep breaths worthy of Tubeman – STRAIGHT GIN! Could anyone in this classroom say which is which?

My friend Robert Anderson could, and did: The animated were in the jar of water, and the others were in the gin – and, yes, these dormant ones, all of them, to a worm, were dead. Someone clapped then, and everyone else joined in; and to this day I am not entirely sure how much, or what part in particular, of what we had heard and seen we were applauding.

My truck and I were approaching the depot, nearing the side road that led to the elevator, when I heard something solid against the running board. It was Myron Bateman, leaning down, grinning into my face, happy as a lark, sober as a judge. He motioned me out of the cab, and with large and equal amounts of relief and gratitude I complied. Mr. Bateman stuffed three shiny quarters in the bib of my overalls, thanked me, slapped me on the shoulder, and jumped into the cab behind the wheel, where (and there was no doubt in my mind about this) he belonged.

I crossed the street to the sidewalk and headed north. Hadsall's Champlin station. Trotter's hole-in-the-wall. Trent's shoe repair. The Rialto.

No need to spend any of my three quarters, unless I want some popcorn. I have enough free passes, by way of my mowing Mr. Shutt's buffalo grass, to last me all the way into Christmas.

It's Betty Grable in *Coney Island*. Yes, Mr. Earl W. Shutt, I have seen this movie before, several times. Cesar Romero and Phil Silvers. Yes, I know, it should have been titled *Corny Island*. But aren't Miss Grable's legs in Technicolor too divine not to be seen again – then again? And that fireandbrimstone lipstick on her fireandbrimstone lips? And Miss Lulu from Louisville – was there ever such an animated rendition?

Yes, I'll have a sack of popcorn, thank you, heavy on the salt. And keep the change.

I enter the darkened theater halfway through the main feature, already drunk as a lord.

8

HERE'S THE PROBLEM: My grandfather's farm, all of it – hill and rock and manifold gumbo – has been invaded by a horde of rabbits, both cottontail and jack, and there seems to be no end to their numbers. They are threatening to devour the entire quarter section, including the rocks.

Here's the hoped-for solution: two .12-gauge shotguns, one a single, the other a double, barrel.

Early in December my father received a letter from Grandfather asking him to spend Christmas weekend on the farm, during which time they would conduct what he called a "rabbit roundup." With the .12-gauge shotguns the two would somehow manage to surround the invaders and would force, at the least, a retrograde movement or, at the most, annihilation. Grandfather would hock his underwear, if necessary, he said, or words to that effect, to lay in a bountiful supply of ammunition.

Father, to the surprise of his family, replied, Yes. And as reinforcements he would bring his platoon of wife and daughter and two sons with him.

At home in Attica, in a wood-frame house the equivalent of a matchbox, the Kloefkorns warmed themselves over an ongoing fire of anticipation. A bitter cold winter would have impended had it not already swept down upon us; the temperature dipped to zero and stayed there. But, so far, neither ice nor snow. And if we were to be deterred, it would be the doing of ice or snow, or both, not the coldness by itself. We crossed our fingers and waited.

Our luck held. No ice. No snow.

We loaded the trunk of the Ford with more gear than it could hold, including extra coats and caps and gloves and heavy socks, and headed east. This time the axle failed to break; this time Father was deprived of any opportunity to clench his teeth and perform a ritual largely composed of invectives. We sailed down and up and over the narrow highway without encountering the slightest impediment, not even a headwind. My sister studied the passing landscape in lovely, sisterly silence. My little brother dozed. Father whistled snatches of "The Great Speckled Bird." My mother looked justifiably pleased. And I sat trying to imagine the immensity of a rabbit roundup. How many rabbits, after all, might there be? Grandfather's vow to hock his underwear, or words to that effect, notwithstanding, would he have enough money to buy enough ammunition to put an end to the infestation? And were the jackrabbits as big or as plentiful as his letter had claimed?

Without a riffle our flagship sailed through the main street of Anthony before tacking the outskirts of Bluff City and Caldwell. On, then, to South Haven, our arrival at its shore meaning that soon we would see the beaches of Arkansas City, meaning that our arrival at the rabbit-infested farm southwest of Cedar Vale would be not only possible but imminent.

It is a singular joy to have a plan that seems to be working. *What a beautiful thought I am thinking, concerning the great speckled bird.* . . . We arrived at the foot of Grandfather's driveway, I am guessing, on schedule, and Grandfather was there with his team of horses to greet us, in case the flagship had trouble navigating the driveway's rather steep incline or its ruts or its several insidious rocks. What I now believe, if I hadn't believed it then, is that Grandfather had no doubt that the black Ford could negotiate the driveway; he simply enjoyed harnessing his beloved horses, especially when he knew that he was not headed for the field, a two-bottom plow attached to a singletree, but to the foot of the driveway to meet his son and his son's alert detachment of reinforcements.

We negotiated the driveway without incident, Grandfather's beautiful, mile-wide horses beside us, at our left, until almost too soon we arrived at the unpainted farmhouse, where on a space of reasonably level ground beneath a barren black walnut tree Father parked the flagship.

And before I had a chance to shake my grandfather's hand I saw something the size if not exactly the shape of a bear loping up the hill west of the farmhouse. Yes, Grandfather said when he squeezed my hand, my saucer eyes no doubt having conveyed my thoughts, that's a jackrabbit. We will go after him in the morning.

In the morning. Jesus. *We will go after him in the morning.* How could I possibly wait until morning?

Before making the drive to the farm I had had a problem of my own – not marauding rabbits, certainly, but a problem nonetheless: I had needed someone to deliver the morning *Hutchinson Herald* over the Christmas holidays. My mother, bless her, had thought of this problem shortly after Father had replied to Grandfather's request, and it was also my mother, bless her, who solved the problem. Or, to state it more accurately, it was Mother who enabled me to solve the problem myself by making a very difficult choice: keep delivering the *Herald* or trade it for a different route, one that would require a late afternoon delivery, one that would involve the scattering of the *Wichita Beacon*.

Yes, I had said, but if I swap routes I'll still have to find someone to deliver the *Beacon* while I'm at Grandfather's.

No, Mother said, because I have contacted someone who wants the *Herald* route and who, if you trade with him, will deliver both the *Herald* and the *Beacon* while you're gone.

It was not always an easy thing to keep pace with my mother's way of doing things. That is, she would take almost any problem and somehow – intricately, most often – manage to solve it, then having explained both the problem and the potential solution she would leave it to you to make the final determination. Her Socratic method was made possible chiefly because of her amicability and her workplace; as a cook in a cafe she knew everyone and everyone's dog, and she talked with them freely and often – and she was not afraid to ask questions, was not afraid, if the circumstance in her judgment demanded it, to pry.

I knew the boy she had in mind – no, already had *con-tac-ted*. He wanted the *Herald* route, no doubt – though it had fewer customers than did the *Beacon* route – because it would give him time in the afternoons and early evenings to work at a second job.

Swapping routes with him would give me a couple of advantages. For one thing, I'd not have to get out of bed each morning before sunrise; I would not have to leave the bedroom with the image of my little brother warm and asleep burned against my heavy-lidded eyes. And, next, I would be free to go to Grandfather's farm to engage in the rounding up of rabbits.

But there was also, alas, a distinct disadvantage, one that over the next fifty years would become increasingly clear: I would not be spending nearly as much time in Urie's barber shop, where the opportunities for a liberal arts education presented themselves each morning after I had finished the paper route. It is one thing to read about war in Europe and on the beaches of Guadalcanal and Saipan, Guam and Tinian, but it is quite a different thing to hear that same war discussed by those who have insights perhaps keener than General Montgomery, say, or Generals Eisenhower and MacArthur, and who are occasionally willing to extend their perceptions to include other conflicts, such as baseball or sex.

Virgil Schmidt's forecast in June, for example, that the Cardinals and the Browns would be playing a strictly St. Louis Series.

It stands to reason, Virgil said when the series began. It just stands to reason. Whereupon, leaving that conclusion to explain itself, he predicted that the Cardinals would win the Series, and when that indeed occurred Virgil said, It stands to reason. But this time he elaborated. It was the Cooper brothers, he said. Those boys are magic with pants on. Mort Cooper. He has a rag arm. And his brother Walker? Nothing gets past this fellow's glove. Shitfire. Nothing.

Virgil has a very deep voice. When he says *shitfire* the barber shop trembles. Leland Bonham says he read somewhere that Jane Russell went somewhere to help dedicate a new airplane. Or maybe, Leland says, rededicate an old one. I saw her in the *Outlaw*. She could fix my supper for me any old time.

And Yamamoto, Cloyd Stocker says, wasn't that fartknocker educated at Harvard?

I wouldn't go to Harvard if you paid me, says Andy Martin, who is the town drayman.

Give some credit to Brecheen, too, says Urie, meaning Harry the Cat Brecheen, who won game four of the Series. And what about Musial?

And did you read what the Fuhrer said about the war? asks Leland. He must think God is a fucking Nazi.

Hitler's little speech had been in some recent papers and magazines. He said, How could a struggle which has behind it all the fanaticism of a nation end otherwise than in victory, quite irrespective of what the situation may be at the moment?

At the moment, Virgil says, the Fuhrer has ants in his pants.

I don't believe that all of the Germans are fanatics, Stocker says. Most of them have been hoodwinked.

If I was married to Jane Russell, Leland says, I'd do whatever she told me to do, except die, and I'd probably do that, too.

I loved to sit on the green bench in Urie's shop and listen and learn, and the experience was especially pleasant during the winter days when Urie had the woodstove blazing and the warm air joined the sweet hair tonic aromas and you absorbed all of it because you knew that sooner or later you would need to leave and move out into icy air and probably a north wind, so you strained to make every precious instant count.

Surrendering these moments to someone else would not be easy, but I nonetheless decided to agree to the swap. After the rabbit roundup I would henceforth do my delivering and collecting for the *Wichita Beacon*.

After the handshaking, and after each of us had claimed our sleeping quarters, I went outside with my brother to see whether the rabbits, in their numbers, were equal to Grandfather's billing. The sun was setting behind the hill, casting interminable shadows behind us, and in front of us everything looked more or less the color of rabbit – dry bunchgrass, splotches of brown-to-yellow soil, here and there a scrub cedar, plum bushes that in summer bore fruit too tough and bitter for any taste finer than a vulture's. And of course the rocks, some flat, some rounded, some small, some large as baby buildings, many of them in the waning light taking on the aspects of rabbits.

As we had been unloading the Ford – Christmas gifts to the living room, suitcases to their respective bedrooms – Grandfather spoke of the damage the rabbits had inflicted during the summer on both field and garden, how he had fought them with shotgun and, encircling the garden, a fence of chicken wire that the rabbits chuckled and scoffed at until their sides ached, then crawled under to devastate the peas and the corn and the tomatoes and the leafy tops of the potatoes until some of them were too sated to crawl away under the chicken wire, whereupon Grandfather sprayed them with his double-barrel – but of course the next day they were in the garden again, probably even those that he had sprayed the day before, so he had to kill them, some of them, all over again, so that he determined that nothing short of an all-out campaign would serve to discourage them, and that's what we are going to launch, he had said, or words to that effect, beginning tomorrow morning.

Then suddenly Johnny and I saw a jackrabbit – saw it at precisely the same time, shouted and pointed at the same time, followed it then with our shouting and pointing until it lost itself in the shadow of a faraway rock. My brother and I had seen rabbits before, of course, and even jacks; but we had never seen a rabbit to rival the one that had only moments ago galloped into, then out of, our collective ken. Ten years later I would think of this moment as I'd sit reading Mark Twain's incomparable account of a similar experience as he made his way from Missouri to Nevada:

As the sun was going down [he was in Nebraska, at this point, about one hundred and eighty miles from where he had started his journey], we saw the first specimen of an animal known familiarly over two thousand miles of mountain desert – from Kansas clear to the Pacific Ocean – as the "jackass rabbit." He is well named. He is just like any other rabbit, except that he is from one third to twice as large, has longer legs in proportion to his size, and has the most preposterous ears that ever were mounted on any creature but a jackass. When he is sitting quiet, thinking about his sins, or is absentminded or unapprehensive of danger, his majestic ears project above him conspicuously; but the breaking of a twig will scare him nearly to death, and then he tilts his ears back gently and starts for home. All you can see then, for the next minute, is his long gray form stretched out straight and "streaking it" through the low sage-brush, head erect, eyes right, and ears just canted a little to the rear, but showing you where the animal is, all the time, the same as if he carried a jib. Now and then he makes a marvelous spring with his long legs, high over the stunted sagebrush, and scores a leap that would make a horse envious. Presently he comes down to a long, graceful "lope," and shortly he mysteriously disappears. He has crouched behind a sagebush, and will sit there and listen and tremble until you get within six feet of him, when he will get underway again. But one must shoot at this creature once, if he wishes to see him throw his heart into his heels, and do the best he knows how. He is frightened clear through, now, and he lays his long ears down on his back, straightens himself out like a yard-stick every spring he makes, and scatters miles behind him with an easy indifference that is enchanting.

My brother and I stood looking at each other for some time, each of our faces, I am certain, absolutely devoid of everything but disbelief. Had we actually seen what we thought we saw? A jackrabbit the size of an honest-to-goodness bear?

Perhaps because as the sun continued to set everything on the hillside was becoming darker, or perhaps because deep down we believed that what we had seen was not a delusion, we did not walk to the boulder where the jack had disappeared to further document its existence. Our curiosities satisfied, we returned to the farmhouse.

Where the cracks in the range in the kitchen were aflame and the air and the general atmosphere were synonymous with supper. Grandmother, though weakened by the first stage of a cancer that before the end of next year would bring her down, was well aproned and well into giving the boiled potatoes a thorough spanking. The table was thickly set. Two or three leghorns lay beautifully dismembered, each member brown and sizzling in black iron skillets, each skillet, following the lifting out of the legs and the thighs and the wings and the breasts, abubble with gravy. Jesus. Wash your hands, boys, someone admonished, and we did. We had seen the bear veiled thinly as a rabbit, and we could feel our ribs beginning to tickle our backbones. We were ready to eat.

Make a wish, Mother said, and I closed my eyes and wished that the evening might pass quickly to permit the rabbit roundup to proceed, and when the wishbone snapped and I saw that I was holding the larger half, I was delighted. And indeed my wish was granted. Evening moved swiftly into night, night swiftly into time for bed.

Too swiftly, because Grandfather had dusted off his old red-and-black accordion and, its bellows leaking, had played several hymns, among them "In the Sweet By and By" and "Onward, Christian Soldiers." The latter seemed especially relevant in view of the upcoming massacre of rabbits. He sang with gusto, his thick fingers working the keyboard, the creaking of his rocker providing a regular though somewhat discordant accompaniment. *Like a mighty army moves the church of God; brothers, we are treading where the saints have trod. . . .*

We were all of us in the living room, the largest room in the farmhouse but, even so, not very large; not far from the north wall sat the woodstove, its black pipe with its damper open hot to the touch I had earlier applied, the pipe's top disappearing into the ceiling, a pyramid of hedgewood at the ready nearby. A duofold rested along the west wall; commodious and covered with well-worn leather, it would be the bed my grandmother would die on, refusing all forms of medication, insofar as she had the strength. Grandfather would sleep on a pallet of quilts on the floor beside her. He would be thankful that she died in her sleep.

But at the moment she was sitting in her own rocker not far from the doorway to the kitchen, in case Grandfather's showmanship went beyond the limits of Scripture, which I assume it didn't: Grandmother remained in her rocker all evening, slightly rocking, at times humming along with Grandfather's singing, and when he moved from hymn to recitation she stayed where she was, though she appeared more stoic than pleased. *And there was Ham and there was Shem and there was Japheth, ah, and they all ran into the ark, ah,* my sister sitting cross-legged on the floor beside me, her giggling making me giggle, and my brother, too, Mother and Father sitting not far away on straight-backed wooden chairs brought in from the kitchen. The scene was lighted by a brace of lamps, one on a small end table near the duofold, the other on an ancient oak library table whose middle drawer housed tablets and pencils and on whose low shelf rested a large black Bible. The lamplight flickered from time to time, though Grandfather had trimmed the wicks as Grandmother washed and toweled the globes. The farmstead had no electricity, or running water, because my German grandfather had a stubborn streak in him, according to more than one of his children, approximately a mile wide.

When Grandfather began to recite another story I thought I saw Grandmother flinch, but perhaps the lamplight was playing tricks; in any case, she remained in her rocker and the story continued – the one we found even more amusing than that of Noah and his ark, the one of the farmer and his possessive hen.

And so it was that the night went by too quickly, my wish unfortunately granted. Even so, I went to bed without much protesting. I would need a good night's rest before the shooting began in the morning. So I left it to Grandfather to adjust the damper and bank the fire and blow out the lamps. Then, too, I knew what the bedroom had to offer – a bed with a feather mattress at least two fathoms deep, with hand-tied quilts enough to keep me securely in place as they kept me warm. Because the old farmhouse, like the bellows on Grandfather's accordion, was leaking air, and before I had removed my shoes and socks already I had begun to shiver.

Up rose the sun, wrote Chaucer in the *Knight's Tale*, and up rose Emily.

And so did my father and grandfather, though to my knowledge neither had ever been accused of playing the role of nonpareil in a chivalric romance. They had milked the cows, all four of them, and had slopped the hogs and fed hay to the horses before they came into the bedroom to shake me and my brother into consciousness. And put on your long johns, Father said, or you'll freeze to death.

During the night the temperature, already cold, had dropped considerably, and when I looked out the window I saw almost nothing but an immaculate layer – four inches deep as it turned out – of snow. Many of the smaller rocks had been buried, and snow lay beautifully bright on the tops of the larger stones, including turtle rock. I had slept in my long johns, and my brother in his, so we went right to work fumbling our way into socks and shirts, sweaters and overalls, ankle-high boots and caps with earflaps that we were instructed to remove as we tackled breakfasts of ham and eggs and biscuits and leftover gravy over toast, all washed down with tall glasses of fresh milk whiter than snow.

Sound sleep is surely high on the list of human blisses. John Neihardt, in *All Is But a Beginning*, rates what he calls "deep sleep" fourth on his list of human "goods," close on the heels of love – "love given," as he puts it, "rather than love received," followed by "the satisfaction of the instinct of workmanship," and trailing that, in the third position, "the exaltation of expanded awareness in moments of spiritual insight." He offered this list in response to a question and some assertions proffered by a somewhat cynical young friend. "What's good about this absurd predicament in which we find ourselves? We don't know whence we came; we don't know where we are; we don't know whither we are bound. It is hard to come here, hard to remain, and hard to get away."

At Grandfather's farm that morning, having indulged several hours of deep sleep, I knew where I was – in the kitchen, wolfing breakfast. I had come from Attica, Kansas, one hundred and twenty miles to the west. And it had been, this time anyway, a journey free of hardnesses. Remaining here would be nothing short of undiluted pleasure, though leaving here would be, yes, hard. Absurd predicament? Pshaw. Go speak of absurd predicament to all those rabbits we were at the brink of bringing down.

I had slept so soundly, in fact, that I hadn't heard a single peep from any quarter. While Father and Grandfather were doing chores, Grandmother and Mother were assembling breakfast, Grandfather having started fires in both the woodstove in the living room and the range in the kitchen. All of this activity, the thudding of hedge-logs, the sizzling of ham and the clattering of plates and cups and saucers, had taken place as my brother and I lay soundly asleep, snug as infants in the featherbed arms of Morpheus.

Our sister meanwhile lay asleep on the duofold. She slept as we consumed breakfast, and she was sleeping when my brother and I, fully capped and coated, stepped onto the south porch to join Father and Grandfather for the roundup.

Oh, but the morning was grand! Whatever shortcomings the acreage might have had before the snowfall were gone now, covered with a blanket whiter than cows' milk. Father and Grandfather were standing on the south porch near the separator, checking their weapons. They too were bundled to the hilt, their coat pockets bulging with ammunition. If Grandfather had found it necessary to hock his underwear to buy shells, the underwear must have sold for far more than a pretty penny, because extra boxes of shells lay stacked knee-high to an elephant on the floor in the northwest corner.

The porch we stood in abutted the house, its windows on the west and south made of screen, the wall to the east the same that provided the west wall of the living room. From the house you entered the porch through a door to the kitchen. From the porch you went outside through a screen door, and it is this screen door that at last we opened to begin the roundup – Grandfather with the single-barrel, Father with the double, my brother and I prepared – gloves on our hands – to stack the bodies of the rabbits atop the cave just west of the porch. Thus had we been instructed.

I was not prepared for what happened when, trudging uphill through powdery snow, we approached a large thicket of plum bushes. Rabbits of every size and denomination erupted from the bushes, and when the first shell exploded I jumped and covered ears that already my earflaps were covering. More explosions followed, more and then more, because the rabbits, cottontails and jacks, were fleeing uphill in four inches of newly fallen snow, and their movements were scrambled and desperate and in slow motion, giving Father and Grandfather time to take careful aim and to load and reload, until the immediate area was littered with the soft warm corpses of the slain.

This is a welcome snow, Grandfather had said at breakfast. And suddenly I was beginning to understand what he had meant.

In a state of semishock I went to work mopping up the battlefield, Johnny beside me toting his own fair share of the vanquished. The bodies of the rabbits were unbelievably limp, and some of them, the jacks most certainly, so heavy we occasionally were reduced to invectives in order to see them all the way to the top of the cave, *Jesus!* and *Shit on the pump handle!* being perhaps the most popular and effective, the latter a new one I had borrowed from an enlightened snooker player in Butch Mischler's recreation parlor.

Soon enough a procedure evolved, which I suppose is common enough when one is engaged in open warfare. Father and Grandfather, having decimated one thicket, would pause long enough to examine the bores of their shotguns, and reload them, and maybe say a sentence or two about the success of their offensive push or comment on the briskness of the weather before moving on to another thicket. My brother and I would meanwhile continue our lugging and our stacking; at the start we had determined to count the bodies, but when after more than a few sorties we disagreed on the tally we decided to count them later when, as forewarned, we would load them into gunny sacks to be delivered to a neighbor who would process them by cutting them into small pieces to feed his minks.

I didn't know what minks were, so Grandfather had explained them, or tried to; they were small animals that could be raised in captivity for considerable profit, their lovely fur in demand for the making of stoles and such, and because I didn't know what a stole was, either, I nodded wisely, though it did seem strange to me that a farmer, who like Grandfather must have spent most of his time milking cows and plowing ground and nursing hogs and chickens, should be feeding dead rabbits to small animals in cages, animals whose systems turned the dead rabbits into fur stoles and such. Are there some things, after all, that young boys are not meant to understand?

There seemed to be no end to the thickets, or to the rabbits that spilled from them, or to large rocks, either, from behind which also the rabbits fled, their fleeing of course, for the most part, futile. Because my brother and I constituted the cleanup detail, we were far enough away so that the blasts from the shotguns did not set us back on our heels, as was the case with the initial explosion. I tell you, whoever you are or hope to become, there is no sound quite like the sound of a .12-gauge clearing its throat on a frigid, windless, early morning on a hillside southwest of Cedar Vale, Kansas, after a four-inch snowfall. And nothing quite like the smell of the gunsmoke, potassium nitrate and sulfur, that hangs forever cumulus in the bright icy air.

Or the relentless weight of rabbits, though dead, dragging you down.

Or the bright polar air causing your cheeks to tingle, until you begin to wonder if ice might not be a harsher afterlife punishment than fire.

But it was the rabbits, I believe, one moment alive, the next a consortium of red flesh and sinew, fur and intestine and eyes astonishingly clear that caused me to grow heartsick of the entire operation. I didn't say anything, of course, because I knew that in spite of my squeamishness we were doing what had to be done. The rabbits were eating my grandparents out of house and home, as Grandfather had said, and therefore they must be brought down.

So with my brother, whose stamina impressed me, I followed the hunters and heard the explosions from their .12-gauges and smelled their gunsmoke and toted the bewildered victims to their place atop the cave and looked at the blood on my gloves and trudged back for another helping. And in spite of the exercise, which kept me warm under my coat and shirt and long johns, my cheeks continued to tingle.

Twice Johnny and I returned to the porch to fetch more shells, and before they had been expended our procedure had evolved to a routine that excluded even the smallest shred of sympathy or concern. Or, to put it another way: To hell with the rabbits. They were, after all, only rabbits, only food for the minks, and apparently, like the common sparrow, they were too numerous to lose sleep over.

And I didn't, and neither did Johnny. Somewhere at the edge of Sister Hook's eternity the campaign ended, whereupon I made a beeline for the bedroom, where, shadowed by my brother, I dumped my clothes, exclusive of long johns, and crawled back into bed, securing a fistful of hand-tied quilt snugly at the chin. Johnny the shadow was not far behind. Throughout the campaign he had insisted upon designations – Nips for the cottontails, Krautheads for the jacks. I had humored him, he being a youngster who didn't yet know starboard from port, feces from Shinola.

Before the feather mattress had had time to envelop us entirely, we were, collectively and otherwise, dead to the world.

9

A STORY IN THE *Wichita Beacon* described the movements of the Allied forces as inexorable. *In-ex-o-ra-ble. Adj. Not to be persuaded or moved by entreaty. Relentless.* The movement thus far had indeed been inexorable, I suppose, though folding the papers day after day in Hadsall's Champlin station I thought *never-ending*, as in eternal, might have been more accurate. Does God draw straight with crooked lines? Does He draw with any lines whatsoever? Was the cynic in Neihardt's book perhaps correct after all? We don't know whence we came, he had said; we don't know where we are, and we don't know whither we are bound. It is hard to come here, hard to remain, and hard to get away.

Yet the movements of the Allied forces were inexorable, and they were headed for Paris and Berlin; the troops had come from many diverse places, including Kansas, and, yes, the marches to Paris and Berlin were difficult, as some of the photos in the *Beacon* so graphically illustrated, but the movements were relentless, the paper said, which meant that eventually victory with a capital V would happen – wouldn't it?

Yes, but not as soon as General Eisenhower had predicted, not until May, not until our lexicons had been expanded by the awful music of *buzz-bomb* and *Wehrmacht* and *Gotterdammerung* and *blitzkreig* and . . .

And then *inexorable* had its day. It arrived a month after I had delivered the *Beacon* photo of President Roosevelt soaking his feet in the curative waters at Warm Springs, Georgia, those magic waters nonetheless unable to prevent his death, and after the fire-bombing of Dresden, an action that one individual said was not meant to destroy military installations, there being no military forces or military installations in Dresden, but was instead an action intended to "un-house" the civilians at Dresden, to let them know that the destruction wrought by their Luftwaffe had not been for-gotten.

And then, inexorably, another harvest came and went, and a pretty good one, too, according to the men in the pool hall, one of whom saw it as a favorable omen, a precursor to the defeat of Japan. And what, finally, is the recipe for an Allied victory? Simple, said a domino player. You follow Admiral Bull Halsey's strategy. You kill Japs, kill Japs, and then kill more Japs.

I too had a plan, one that came to me back in May, shortly after I graduated from the seventh grade. It came to me a few minutes after I walked into Skeet Lew's five-and-dime to collect for the *Beacon*, and it came in the form of a portable Philco radio with a carry-ing handle and a covering that resembled honest-to-God brown leather. It was roughly twice the size of the .50-caliber ammo box sitting near Robert Taylor and his machine gun at the end of the movie as the sergeant, grinning defiantly and squeezing the trigger like a madman, was being overrun by a relentless horde of Japanese.

I saw that radio, the only one of its kind in the store, and I wanted it too much not to buy it. My mother would have said I wanted it so much I could taste it.

Skeet Lew, a thin, kind man who had two sons I liked to shoot baskets with, must have read both my mind and my mother's tongue. I'll put it away for you, he said, and you can pay for it in installments. I nodded. Mr. Lew took the radio to a small room at the back of the store. And bingo! I owned a new Philco radio, more or less. I was dizzy.

And the amazing thing is that Mother, hearing the news, did not disapprove. Nor did my father, who received the news by way of my mother. I would pay for the radio, I told them, in three installments – one at the end of the first week in June, another at the end of the first week in July, and the final payment early in August. What I did not mention was that I intended to spend my thirteenth birthday on the twelfth of August holed up in my bedroom listening all day to whatever the magic of radio had to offer.

I now believe that my parents were wise far beyond my twelve-year-old perceptions of them. They no doubt were pleased that their older son had committed himself to something more stable than the playing of pinball machines or the shooting of pool or the buying of copies of *Wonder Woman* and the *Torch and Toro*. Their older son had a plan that would require discipline and frugality, and the fruits of these would be far sweeter, they must have believed, and more enduring, than mere earthly pleasures.

And here is another amazing thing: They were correct. I made the first payment on schedule and so, too, the second. And when I went into the five-and-dime to complete the transaction I was excited beyond description. And when I saw Mr. Lew walking toward me with the Philco under his right arm I believe that I vowed never again to squander another red cent, but instead to buy radios, or their lovely equivalents, until the day I died.

But Skeet Lew, having handed me the radio, would not accept the final payment.

It's already paid for, he said. Your mother was in the store several days ago. She said to tell you happy birthday.

I don't remember whether I said anything, but I do remember that I looked at Mr. Lew for what seemed a long time, looked him in the eyes, which were brown as the leather on the Philco, and probably I nodded several times, but only slightly, and probably Mr. Lew was surprised that I didn't perform a cartwheel or at least let loose an appreciative groan or gasp, or maybe he could tell by looking at my own eyes, which are almost as green as my father's, that I was appreciative beyond groan or gasp – I don't know. But he smiled, and I left the store holding its handle, the right front pocket of my jeans fat with all those beautiful bills that thanks to my beautiful mother I didn't have to spend.

I always enjoy the banter that takes place in Urie's; so when I deliver the *Beacon* to the barber shop I make it a point to hang around for a few minutes or, on Saturday, to spend maybe an hour or so listening and watching and browsing J. G. Taylor Spink's *Sporting News*.

Urie is pleased that his Dodgers are leading the National League.

Don't start celebrating yet, Leland Bonham says. Look out for them Cubs. They have Claude Passeau.

Piss on Claude Passeau, says Virgil Schmidt.

Urie smiles. He has shaved enough throats, I'm guessing, to be able to handle libel.

Detroit has Newhouser, Cloyd Stocker says. The Tigers will take it all.

Piss on Passeau, anyway, Virgil says.

The wondrous thing about Virgil Schmidt is that no matter what he says you take it kindly. It's that low, mellow voice of his, voice at once friendly and authoritative.

Well, says Leland Bonham, don't start celebrating yet.

Apparently Urie chooses not to take Leland's advice, because he lays his razor on the shelf behind him and walks briskly to the back room where abides his means of celebration, his bottle of ardent spirits. The man lying on his back in the big chair has closed his eyes. One side of his face is clean shaven, the other side thickly lathered. Asleep or awake, one thing is certain: He must be patient.

For the record, our viewing of the nightcrawlers in Miss Vermilia's classroom, those worms both alive and those eternally snockered, had not officially ended the ladies' presentation. To provide a formal closure they recited what they claimed were Carry A. Nation's favorite temperance lines:

Touch not, taste not, handle not:
Drink will make the dark, dark blot.
Like an adder it will sting,
And at last to ruin bring
Those who tarry at the brink.

Having recited these cherished lines, the crusaders in black repeated them, but this time as a song, and insofar as two husky women can constitute a full-blown choir they were indeed full-blown, if not a choir, their faces rife with expression, their harmony close enough to be counted. Before this benediction began, the ladies had given each of us a small wooden hatchet as a remembrance, after which they distributed what they called "pledge cards" and asked us to read them and then to sign them, if we so chose; and, praise the Lord, they hoped sincerely that we would so choose, because that is what both they and God wanted us to do.

I read the black words on my card. They called for the signer to pledge, by way of a signature, never to use tobacco in any form or indulge the drinking of what Native Americans many moons ago called the Water That Warms You.

I didn't sign my card right away. I read the pledge, then looked around to see whether my colleagues were moving in any discernible direction. My buddies Evan and R. D. were signing the cards, or so I thought, and most of the girls, having touched the tips of their pencils with the tips of their pretty little tongues – and probably having been influenced by Ruth Crocker, who was a pious ringleader if there ever was one and who was nodding yes, yes, yes – were making their commitments, too, so I scribbled my name on the line at the bottom of the card and folded it and slipped it into the bib pocket of my overalls.

I had hesitated to sign the pledge because I did not want to sever, altogether, a potential relationship with tobacco. "Ardent spirits," the Water That Warms You, would be easy to give up, or never to indulge, because I frankly did not know what the hell, beyond the calming of night crawlers, they might induce. But tobacco was another matter, because recently my father had bought a small miracle that with not much more than a flick of one's wrist would roll a weed almost as tight as the ones sold in Moulton's grocery store. Once in a while my father trusted me with this contraption, with it and a sack of Bull Durham and a pack of tissues. He would give me an empty Lucky Strike container, say, and instruct me to fill it with roll-your-owns, whereupon he would leave me to do the work without his supervision.

Faith. Faith is what a father has when he leaves his young son alone with tobacco and tissues and a small miracle capable of manufacturing cigarettes that honest-to-Betsy might pass as store-bought. (It also is what a small son has when on a snowy day he goes to sleep in the back seat of the family Ford, when he drifts into nothingness believing that his father at the wheel will deliver him, and his mother and brother and sister, safely to his grandfather's rocky farm.) And it was a combination of things that led me into temptation, into yielding then to a puff or two, then into the purloining of an entire cigarette. The initial lure was the aroma of the tobacco, a sweet olfactory sensation that no reasonable fourth-grader could ignore or deny. A second lure was the firmness, the neatness of the end product, as mentioned above. A third, and probably this was the deciding factor – though a fourth, the imitating of a father's habit, no doubt carried some weight – was the taste of tissue and tobacco as I licked the seam to secure it. You move the moist tip of your tongue along that seam, slowly and carefully, and the gustatory pleasure is enough to send you to the kitchen for matches, if your mother is safely somewhere else.

So I had been reluctant to sign the pledge card, to pledge away not the temptation but the yielding, but at last I did, and so did the others, or most of them, and we were told to keep the cards and to respect our pledges and to remember Carry A. Nation, and they recited, then sang, Carry's favorite temperance lines, and when I returned to the room from recess the ladies in black were gone and with them the photograph of Sister Nation and all traces of the jars and the water and the night crawlers and everyone's mortal enemy, demon rum.

What I hadn't realized, of course, is that while the crusaders were killing worms and speaking of Carry A. Nation and harmonizing, half a world away the Japanese were planning an attack on Pearl Harbor, fireandbrimstone and the USS *Arizona* with its crew going down, forever down, and soon enough tobacco would be difficult to come by, and the magic roll-your-own machine would sit on a shelf bereft of the Bull Durham it needed to perform its wonders, and in a year or so I would have misplaced my pledge card and thus would be forced to smoke Folgers rolled in toilet paper, R. D. and I sitting outside at the back of the Rialto facing the alley, enjoying our coughing and our watering eyes to the utmost.

And perhaps, had the ladies in black been given more time, they would have told us about Carry's three favorite hatchets, weapons she named affectionately Faith, Hope, and Charity, or maybe they could have sung a song that she composed herself as Mother Goose looked over one shoulder:

Sing a song of six joints,
With bottles full of rye;
Four and twenty beer kegs,
Stacked up on the sly.
When the kegs were opened,
The beer began to sing,
Hurrah for Carry Nation,
Her work beats anything.

At times, too, her words more than matched her work. Perhaps, had the ladies from the WCTU been given additional time, they might have mentioned at least two of Mrs. Nation's pithier observations, the first an oblique reference to tobacco – "It is horrible that a woman will consent to kiss a walking spittoon" – and the second a not-so-oblique reference to John Barleycorn: "Liquor is a bad thing, but it seems that people find it out like hogs find slop – each one has to burn his own individual snout."

These are strong words, perhaps too strong for the ears of fourth-graders, as was Sister Nation's plea for young folks actively to join her cause:

My Precious Little Children: – I send you greetings and ask you to help me destroy that which is on the streets and protected by the police and the city officials to destroy you, my darlings. I want every one of you little ones to grab up a rock and smash the glass doors and windows of these hell-holes. You will do your duty and enroll your name on the pages of undying fame, and place your self on the side of God and humanity.

Or, finally – time and incentive permitting – the ladies might have told us something of the tireless range of Carry A. Nation's exploits, those corridors of chaos that took her beyond Kiowa and Wichita to Des Moines, Chicago, St. Louis, Canada, Massachusetts, Cincinnati, Rochester, Buffalo, Yale and Harvard and Cambridge, Indiana and Kentucky and Michigan, Houston, Denver, Glasgow, London, Arkansas, West Virginia, New Jersey, Maine, to Cleveland and to a wagonload of Kansas hamlets, including Scott City and Anthony and Salina, Chanute and Arkansas City and Garden Plain and, most notoriously, Topeka, where her "hatchetations," as she called them, created mayhem of the highest order, and where she spent many nights in jailhouses, praying for and preaching to the inmates – and, finally, to Leavenworth, where on June 2, 1911, she died, this Hatchet Woman of Medicine Lodge, having whispered, slowly, I – have – done – what – I – could.

With hands steadied by firewater, by the Water That Warms You, Urie shaves the lathered half of his customer's face. I am beginning to believe that the customer, Andy Martin, the town drayman, is indeed asleep, he is that silent, that motionless.

When this war ends, says Stocker, I'm buying me a new Buick with whitewall tires.

Make mine a Plymouth, says Virgil.

No, says Leland, I'll settle for a Chevy.

What you intend to use for collateral? asks Stocker.

My good looks, says Leland.

I like Andy Martin. He is not a very clean man, wearing as I am sure he does the same pair of overalls from one work-weary week into another. And his attitude toward personal hygiene seems to have carried over to his wife and their countless children, all of them draymen, in one form or another, all of them preoccupied, it seems, with collecting and shuffling and reshuffling trash that the father for reasons I don't understand hasn't hauled away. Their unpainted house, therefore, and the corner lot it sits on, is a repository of boxes and cans filled with cans and boxes and Lord only knows what else.

But I like Andy Martin. He is a kind man with a wide, toothless smile, and two or three times a year he'll spend a few precious coins for a shave that must to him be a pleasure akin to – what? To the buying of a new portable Philco radio, maybe, or to the swell anticipation of turning thirteen. And I like Andy Martin because I saw tears in his eyes when he lifted the bloody body of my dog Spunky from beneath the heavy bed of his dump truck.

You keep working at it, Stocker says to Urie, you'll have Andy looking almost like a human being.

He had held Spunky as if cradling a child. Then he offered the little body to me, and I looked down at my brother before I took it. Blood was oozing from Spunky's ears and mouth. He was limp as a wet dishrag.

We called him Spunky because he was a small, black-and-white definition of perpetual motion. He had arrived running and yipping into our backyard one early Sunday afternoon, a stray who apparently appeared from nowhere, and that was that. Johnny and I suddenly owned a dog, and we had not watched him cavort very long before we named him what his antics called for – Spunky.

Urie wipes the last of the lather from Andy Martin's face, covers the face then with a white washcloth made steamy by hot running water. Now Andy is a mummy about to reenter the land of the living.

But Spunky's spunk, alas, took him, many times, into dangerous territory, his fatal exploration occurring as he barked at one of the rotating front wheels on Andy Martin's dump truck.

Andy reached a hand deep into a front pocket and brought forth two fifty-cent pieces.

Here, boys, he said, handing the coins to my little brother. This is what the city pays me to dispose of a dead animal. You might want to bury your dog yourselves. I'm sorry.

There were tears at the corners of Andy Martin's eyes. His face was dirty and he needed a shave – and a haircut, too.

Urie removes the steaming washcloth, towels Andy's face, moves the back of the big chair, and Andy with it, to an upright position.

By God, Virgil says to Andy, Stocker was right. You look almost human.

We buried Spunky in the backyard under the branches of a sprawling elm. The ground was hard and we had to soften it with water we carried in a bucket from an outside faucet. But the water only softened the top of the soil, so we had to continue to carry buckets of water. Later, telling our story, Mother will say that we didn't *dig* a hole so much as we *worried* one, she being perhaps the world's foremost authority on the subject of worrying.

Andy studies himself in the mirror, apparently pleased with what he sees. He does in fact look like a different person. Grinning, he tells Urie that he guesses he'll have a haircut, too.

We finally had worried a hole deep enough to accommodate Spunky. Together we placed him into the hole, then took turns covering him first with dirt, then with clumps of half-brown bunch-grass. The day was hot, even in the shade of the elm, and, having returned the spade to its place in the garage, we went into the house, into the kitchen, for a tall drink of water.

Andy watches himself in the mirror as Urie cuts and trims his long, unruly hair, and I too watch Andy's image as it becomes more and more human. I like Andy Martin. I like the way he changes slowly from a somewhat animal into a more-than-somewhat man. He had given my brother and me two fifty-cent pieces, then climbed into the cab of his old dump truck and with an enormous growl of its engine drove away.

Believe this much: On this particular Saturday afternoon I not only like Andy Martin but I like additionally damn near everything. And why not? I am the owner of a new Philco portable radio. School will not begin for one more full and blessed month. I have a wad of bills, thanks to my beautiful mother, as yet unspent. In eight days I'll turn thirteen. And before I leave Urie's barber shop I too, no less than Andrew Martin, will be a new man.

So jot this down: It is good to be young and alive and free of debt on a warm, bright, windless afternoon in August, nothing but a paper route to disturb the holy tedium, after which a chocolate malt at the Rexall drugstore, after which perhaps a Technicolor fling with Betty Grable at the Rialto, after which some wandering in the pool hall or back at the drugstore, playing the pinball machine or watching as others play, during which time you can read a comic book or two without spending so much as a dime. Then across the street to Moulton's grocery to smell the sawdust as Mr. Moulton sweeps the floor on his way to closing up. Jesus.

Andy steps down from the chair, gives Urie a dollar bill, receives his change without taking his eyes away from the mirror. From the neck up he is a boy, from the Adam's apple down a man – and a dirty man at that, his blue workshirt and his blue overalls bearing the grit and the grime of ages. He grins at the face in the mirror, and the face in the mirror returns the favor.

I like Andrew Martin. With his dump truck he keeps our village more or less spic and span. He had given me and my brother two half dollars. There were tears at the corners of his eyes. With a spade Johnny and I worried a hole in the stubborn south central Kansas ground. Spunky lies in that hole, his small mongrel bones covered with dirt and bunchgrass. Is it any wonder, then, that it is good to be young and alive and free of debt on a warm, bright, windless afternoon in August?

10

FOR THE RECORD, shortly before eleven I left the drugstore and crossed the street to Moulton's grocery, but I did not go there strictly to smell the sawdust. I went there also to watch and admire one of my heroes, Mr. Moulton's son, Johnny, who had survived the landing at Normandy but in the process had been wounded severely in his left leg. He had been treated on the spot, as the story went, the spot being an expanse of wooded acreage not far from Berlin, then to London for treatment, and then, shortly before another Kansas harvest had found its way into the elevator across from the Santa Fe depot, he arrived back home, where with an awkward limp he went to work with his father at the store.

At the store. It was not the only grocery store in town, but Moulton's was the largest and the warmest and the best attended, and to my hero Johnny Moulton it was home. Name it home, my friend the poet says, and *it will live in you no matter where you live no matter how you live as long as you live*.

And the story had it that Johnny survived because he went head first into the ditch, that beside him his buddy did not survive because he went feet first, meaning very simply that Johnny took the rounds in his leg, while his buddy took them in his neck. So tell me this: How was it possible for Johnny's buddy to have been prepared for his death at the hand of a German?

Be in advance of all parting.

Those were not my maternal grandmother's words, certainly; I read them years later in a poem, I believe it was, by Rilke or someone else; in any case, the message, from Rilke or from my grandmother, was the same.

She was a short, wide, thick, opinionated German woman who had come to this country when she was seventeen, homesick for her

143

brother Jake, who had preceded her by two or three years and had homesteaded in Kansas near a small town named Nickerson. There she found him; her homesickness abated, and before she could complete arrangements for her return to Karlshuld, near Munich, she had met my grandfather and had fallen in love, the consequence of which was marriage – and her decision to remain in America.

Their first child was a son, Konrad, their second also a son, Charles, and their third a daughter, my mother, Katie Marie. Grandmother's husband, William John, was sixteen years her senior; he died two years before I was born, leaving Grandmother to spend many years fending for herself. She managed somehow to survive, aided by her three children and by her own frugality. I knew her as a woman whose social graces did not endear her to the multitudes. She had a temper, and she did not hesitate to exercise it – on not only her fellow townspeople but likewise on her children, including her only daughter, who happened to be my mother.

But I knew her also as a grandmother who had the good great sense to dote upon her daughter's older son, and perhaps rightly so. I gave her a daily paper, for example, and did not charge her for it. I often took her to Sunday church and sometimes to Wednesday night prayer meeting. I talked with her at length about whatever she wanted to talk about, and on many nights, especially those before the beginning of a new year, played Parcheesi and dominoes with her, and Chinese checkers, both stuffing ourselves with popcorn and apples and licorice and washing it all down with Kool-Aid. And when occasionally either of us suffered with a head cold we would join each other in the imbibing of a magic elixir – that is, a shot of terpene hydrate with codeine. She was a teetotaler who knew only that this medication was legal (it was sold over the counter at the Rexall drugstore), and that many of her God-fearing neighbors and friends used it – and that it worked miracles. Maybe not with the first shot but probably with the second and assuredly with the third.

One of life's great pleasures is that of watching someone else experience great pleasure. My German grandmother sitting with her grandson at a card table in the living room eating popcorn and playing a game of Parcheesi – what could possibly be more pleasurable? Her square, brown, wrinkled face couldn't stop smiling; it was the sort of absolutely wholesome and self-contented smile made possible only because at other times the face, and what went with it, could be so downright ornery or devious. Wasn't it Mark Twain who said that laughter cannot exist without human misery? Didn't he add that therefore there will be no laughter in heaven?

At such times my grandmother didn't need to anticipate paradise; she had it sitting across from her at the card table. She rolls the dice, and, wouldn't you know it, the right number shows itself and she slides her last doohickey home. She laughs. She is fond of her grandson, but she is maybe equally fond of competition, especially when the eyes on the dice come up in her favor. And would I like another tub of popcorn?

One evening in late July she called to ask me to come over and do her a kindness. I was not very eager to oblige because some thunderheads were forming off to the southwest and they looked ominous. On the plains in Kansas you can sense as well as see, and then smell, an oncoming storm. The clouds were dark, brown into purple into black, and a sun not far from setting made them appear perhaps more threatening than they actually were. I was not afraid that I might be blown away, or that Grandmother might suffer a similar fate; I just wanted to stay where I was, at home with some comic books and my own deep meditations.

But of course I hopped on my bike and pedaled the half dozen blocks to where Grandmother stood on the front porch, waiting. She had spent most of the day outside, tending her garden and her flower beds, and she wanted me to put away the hose and the rake and the hoe and the spade, each in its place in the garage, and then move several flowers in their pots from the front porch, which had no roof, to the back porch, which was both roofed and screened in. I did all of this as quickly and as carefully as possible, especially the moving of the flowers.

By the time I had relocated the final pot the storm struck, and with Grandmother I ducked into the living room, closing the door with the help of a sudden and violent gust of wind. And before you could draw another breath the storm had declared that it meant business, thunder rolling, lightning flashing, wind slapping the rain like buckshot against the windows. *And there was Ham and there was Shem and there was Japheth, ah, and they all ran into Grandmother's ark, ah. . . .*

Soon enough, and to my amazement, Grandmother had set up the card table with its folding chairs and was making ready to whip me at yet another game of Parcheesi – or dominoes or Chinese checkers, I could choose my own brand of poison. But in fact it had not been her breaking out the games that surprised me as much as her nonchalance; she was arranging table and chairs and games as if outside all hell was not actually breaking loose, which it was. I tried not to be unduly concerned, but my earlier belief that we would not be blown away was undergoing an urgent test. The wind seemed to be blowing ever more wildly, and the rain had turned into hailstones, and I thought that at any moment they were going to break the south windows, both of them, and sweep into the living room and put an end to our party, if not our lives.

Then suddenly I heard a rat-a-tat-tatting that caused what little hair Urie had left on my head to stand on end. I had been told that a tornado makes a sound like a freight train approaching; but this was no train. It was a rat-a-tat-tatting, and it persisted until, behold, I identified it for the upstart it was: popcorn popping.

Grandmother won the first game, I the second. I had long since relaxed, thanks in part to my grandmother's serenity; through it all she maintained a placid dignity, an outright sense of confidence, which is perhaps why she won the third game, and the fourth.

She had no fear, and it has taken me half a lifetime to understand why: With the help of her grandson she had put her life into an order that to her made ultimate grassroots sense. The garden hose, looking the part of a large black wreath, rested at its appointed place on a nail in the garage; the hoe and the rake and the spade likewise had found their slots; and the flowers – the begonias, the petunias, the marigolds, the one sweet William – were standing potted in a file on the floor of the screened-in porch, awaiting further instructions.

She was, in other words – or in the words maybe of Rilke – *in advance of all parting*. If the storm blew her into oblivion, she would go there with her garden tended and her flowers and tools where they belonged; moreover, she would go there attended by her grandson, who himself was not eager to visit oblivion but who, sitting with his grandmother, eating apples and popcorn and washing them down with Kool-Aid, was willing to take his chances. You roll the dice, don't you, and the numbers show themselves, and you push your doohickey around the board until somebody wins and somebody loses. The storm meanwhile moves on, as storms do, inexorably.

So Johnny Moulton had rolled the dice, had dived head first into the ditch, and he had won; his buddy, on the other hand, had rolled his own set of dice, had jumped feet-first into the ditch, and had taken several slugs in the neck – or, as one story had it, had been almost decapitated.

De-cap-i-tat-ed. Sitting on an old wooden chair in Moulton's grocery I could not watch Johnny Moulton as he filled orders and worked the cash register without seeing also his buddy, without seeing the effect that the bullets, which I could not see, had on his body: *de-cap-i-ta-tion*. Johnny, little or no time to be in advance of anything, going head first into the ditch; Johnny's buddy, little or no time to be in advance of anything, going feet first. You roll the dice, don't you? Yes, sometimes. But no, not always. Sometimes you don't have time to roll them, or sometimes someone else rolls them for you, and without thinking you jump feet first into a pond that has no bottom.

I had hung around the Rexall drugstore – having hung around the pool hall – until nearly eleven o'clock because, for one thing, the owner of the drugstore was competing mightily at the pinball machine against a formidable opponent, and I didn't want to miss any of the action. The owner was a quiet, good-natured pharmacist who knew how to dispense more types of medication than Kansas law permitted, and into this bargain he was highly skilled at the making of malts and highly talented at the playing of the pinball machine. There were no flippers on the machine in the Rexall drugstore; one influenced the movement of the ball by tapping one's palms against the upper corners of the machine – by tapping them with precisely enough force to help guide the ball without causing the machine to tilt. Doc Bauman could do this with finesse equal to the most professional ballet dancer, though I had never seen such a dancer; he would bend his body this way and that as if it were liquid, and he would tap the upper corners of the machine when they needed tapping, and always the tapping was as gentle or as ungentle as it needed to be, and the balls seemed to know and to appreciate all of this, and they would respond, and bells would ring and lights would flash and the red, white, and blue battleship that was the machine's identifying feature would make noises appropriate, I'm guessing, to a battleship, and Doc's score would be recorded at the lower left-hand corner behind the upright glass, and he would grin and turn to his worthy opponent, Rusty Shannon, and say, Would you like to double the bet, Rusty, or do you have shit down your neck?

Rusty Shannon, as far as I know, never once had shit down his neck, meaning that, yes, he would indeed like to double the bet, which was a lot of money, a half dollar, and he would match Doc's additional quarters with two quarters of his own, then would proceed to take his turn.

And Rusty Shannon at the pinball machine was no slouch. He wasn't as liquid as Doc, but what he lacked in the arena of liquid he made up for in intensity. It was as if Rusty Shannon somehow had the power to *will* each ball where he wanted it to go, though of course he augmented his intensity with his own tapping of the palms against the upper corners of the machine. And something else: Rusty, his teeth clamped tightly together, made optimal use of the invective, or so it appeared to me. The balls therefore seemed to react from fear no less than from gravity.

Ah, the thrill of such high-level competition! I stood between the pinball machine and several racks of comic books, holding a copy of *Wonder Woman* in one hand, the other hand in a pocket of my jeans, counting change. Time moved during those golden moments not only inexorably but astonishingly fast. Doc and Rusty were evenly matched, and each seemed to have an inexhaustible cache of quarters. From time to time I would open the comic book and read a page or two, Wonder Woman with her wide, ammo-proof bracelets deflecting bullets from the pistols of many and varied badasses, but most of the time I watched Doc and Rusty as they danced and cursed and swapped quarters, as the bells dinged and the lights flashed and the red, white, and blue battleship made music that I reckon only a pinball battleship can make.

And lately there was another reason why I spent so much time in the Rexall drugstore. She was a classmate, and she had been hired by Doc Bauman to mix shakes and malts and sodas and to scoop ice cream into dishes and then to top the ice cream with chocolate syrup – or butterscotch or strawberry jam or something else equally mouth-watering. She was petite and frisky, dark-eyed and black-haired, and when she smiled, which was frequently, you just wanted her to go right on smiling.

From my position in front of the racks of comic books I could look across the top of the pinball machine and watch her as she mixed and scooped and delivered her swell concoctions to her fortunate customers. She was the first girl I had ever felt like that about. I liked Betty Grable, and certainly Wonder Woman had her own fair share of charms. But this one was different. And one of these nights, I said to myself, I am going to ask her if I might walk her home.

I went finally from the drugstore to Moulton's grocery, where I found a chair near the front but off to one side, a place where I could watch the goings-on without too much being noticed. And mostly what I noticed was that Johnny Moulton's limp didn't prevent him from moving about the store quickly and efficiently, hustling to one end for canned goods, hustling to the other for bread or crackers or flour or maybe a sack of potatoes. Mr. Moulton, short and balding but with energy akin to his son's, stayed most of the time at the southwest corner of the store where he kept the meat counter supplied and where he weighed and wrapped orders for beef and pork and chicken and cold cuts. From my chair I could see his head bobbing and moving this way and that behind the counter. I had bought the copy of *Wonder Woman* I had been more or less reading in the Rexall drugstore, and I'd open it from time to time and read a page or two, then I'd close it and watch Johnny and his dad and the others in the store, most of them, or maybe all of them, people I knew from church or school, or from Urie's barber shop or the Champlin station or the pool hall or depot or cafe or Skeet Lew's five-and-dime.

I would watch until the last customer left, the last dog died, as they say, and I would stick around to inhale the sawdust that lay freshly scattered on the floor before someone swept it up. Usually it was Mr. Moulton who did the sweeping, but tonight – the old man having lost himself in the refrigerated room behind the meat counter – it was Johnny. Here he comes, with an oversized dustpan and a pushbroom; there he goes, limping, moving the sawdust around and behind the candy display, down the aisle behind the open boxes of vegetables and behind the business counter at the end of which sits the cash register, back then toward me, the pile of sawdust growing larger and larger until he stops to sweep it onto the dustpan that he unloads into a cardboard box. And I see him diving into the ditch, see his buddy beside him jumping, watch as the bullets smack into the leg of one and the neck of the other. Danger – or is it death, or valor? – how it smells like sawdust! And it will be another week before I'll have the chance to smell it again.

II

I'LL SAY IT AGAIN: Chronology has at best a habit of collapsing, of becoming quickly smaller, like the leaky bellows of the old red-and-black accordion as my grandfather squeezed it – or at worst not frankly giving a damn.

When fifty years later I stopped in Wichita to visit my father, I was older than I ever intended to be, my father having established the precedent. He was almost eighty. He lived in a small, wood-frame house cluttered with everything from soup to nuts, and then some. He seemed to be quietly happy with himself and his world, which was essentially his cluttered house, though he yet worked as a night watchman at a lumber yard across the city, midnight until six A.M. I rearranged the clutter until I discovered a chair. I sat down. Father was in the process of buttoning a red plaid shirt. When I asked him how things were going, he said, Pretty good, I guess.

Anything new?

Oh, not much, he said. He tucked the shirttail into his faded jeans. Just the weather.

The weather? What's new about the weather?

He located a chair and sat down. We were in the dining room, which was roughly the size of a closet. I noticed, though, that what appeared to be a new TV sat high on a stand in the northwest corner.

I spend a lot of time now watching the Weather Channel, he said. I bought me a new TV.

I should mention that my father had remarried. His wife was gentle, soft-spoken, kind, patient, devout – and sickly, both in body and mind. So sickly, in fact, that she had gone to live with her only son, who was gentle, soft-spoken, kind, patient, and devout.

We talked about the weather, about the Weather Channel, about the relative merits and demerits of television in general and weather forecasters in particular. My father's bottom-line assessment of forecasters was that they didn't know shit from Shinola. Even so, he watched and listened to them, and he more or less believed what they told him, he said, though more often than not, he said, they prove to have had their heads up their asses. But if they predict a storm, he said, a severe one, and they seem to be pretty sure of themselves – and if the look and the feel of conditions outside this very house suggest a storm – he'll believe them and not drive across town to the lumber yard. He didn't want to take any chances.

There was a basement under my father's house, unfinished, with dirt walls and a bed that he resorted to when the summer nights became unbearably hot (air conditioning, he said, was too goddam expensive and too much trouble). In one corner was a bench covered with tools; the remainder of the basement was filled with boxes of nails, screws, check stubs, receipts, catalogs, bolts – everything an old man could collect.

Six months later I visited again.

I asked, How are things with the Weather Channel?

Oh, all right, I guess, he said.

Anything new beyond the weather?

He thought about this. He frowned. Finally he said, Yes, there is. I have taken to drinking.

I was genuinely stunned. My father, who had never imbibed, had *taken to drinking*.

He attempted a devilish grin, but it didn't quite work.

Well, he said at last, no doubt having searched his son's face for some sort of telltale response, what do you think?

Well, I said, I think it's about time.

We talked at some length about the relative merits and demerits of drinking, with occasional side trips into the compelling countryside of weather. I learned that my father had been playing cards from time to time with a neighbor from across the alley and that this neighbor, this neighborly sot, had introduced my father to the manifold pleasures of whiskey – or, to be more precise, of Old Crow whiskey. Father confessed that he now drank one shot each night before going to bed. Helps him into sleep, he said.

There is a long pause, during which time Father, I was about to learn, modified his confession. Then: Well, he said, I'll tell you the truth. Sometimes I have *two* shots before going to bed.

I smiled. I told him that if one shot is good, then surely two are better.

And Zenobia, I said, how is she?

Oh, not good, I guess, he said. I don't see her very often. She doesn't even know me.

She had gone to live with her son because she wanted to be with him at the end, my father said she said, and because my father did not feel either comfortable or competent taking care of her.

The next time I saw my father we were standing at the edge of Zenobia's grave, listening to a Holy Roller preacher – perhaps Sister Hook's grandson – tell us everything, and more, that he had learned at seminary. The weather was blustery and cold, a sudden front – not forecast on the Weather Channel – having moved in to add physical pain to the mental misery being inflicted by the preacher. My brother, Johnny, and my sister, Bernadine, were with us, sharing the gloom. If the preacher should decide eventually to bring a close to his rantings, my father and I planned to go to his house for a change of clothes (his new boots, he said, were killing him), then we would join my brother and his wife at Bernadine's home for lunch. If the preacher . . .

And, wonder of wonders, the preacher did eventually go silent, and I thought of Huckleberry Finn's observation that the best thing about church is how good it feels when it's over.

Back home Father decided to change not only his boots but likewise his shirt and trousers and, while he was at it, elected to do away with his tie. And as he was undergoing this transformation I was supposed to mix each of us a drink.

I had never before mixed my father a drink. When several months ago he confessed to his problem, he had not invited me to have a hand in augmenting it. But now, perhaps owing to the so-lemnity of the occasion, he told me that he would like a shot of Old Crow, and he invited me to join him. He had handed me a jigger in the form of a small fruit jar with a thin band of white adhesive tape near the bottom to mark the appropriate amount, then headed for the bedroom.

I found two glasses, loosened several cubes of ice into them, then began a search for the whiskey. I supposed that it would be some-where in the cupboards, but as I moved from one section to another and saw no Old Crow, I concluded that it must be somewhere else. My father's kitchen was very small, but its clutter rivaled that in the dining room. I would need to confront this clutter and by way of logic and elimination find the bottle of Old Crow.

I looked under the sink. No whiskey. Along the sides and back of the counter. No whiskey. In the refrigerator. No whiskey.

Father came into the kitchen, no doubt expecting whiskey.

Dad, I said, looking him squarely in his grass-green eyes, I can't find the fucking whiskey.

My father grinned. His teeth were not much better than Urie's.

He went to the cupboards, opened a door, and pointed.

Right there, he said.

I looked where he was pointing. Whiskey? Where was it? I looked more closely. And, behold, I saw it, a pint of Old Crow.

At the moment I was not ready to admit why I had not seen the bottle. For one thing (and in my defense), the bottle's front was not entirely facing us; there was chiefly its thin, unlabeled profile. And the main thing: It was only a pint.

The sad truth is that many seasons ago I lost the pledge card that I had signed in Miss Vermilia's fourth-grade class, and the loss had given me permission – or so I must have believed – to imbibe. I therefore imbibed, and it had been a long time since I had pur-chased any amount smaller than a quart. Which means that when the eyes have been catechized to see the quart, they simply do not recognize the existence of the pint. Jesus.

My father and I clinked glasses and sipped our Old Crow, I having used the fruit jar jigger with its white adhesive tape to pour out appropriate amounts. It was a moment of marvelous camaraderie and restraint. We had located our chairs within and among the debris in the dining room. My father looked divinely comfortable in his red plaid shirt and faded jeans, his old boots and his absence of a tie. Zenobia had lived her life and had left it, and her leaving, we concluded, was – all things considered – a blessing, and we better finish these drinks and hurry on over to my sister's house before she gives up on us or, as my mother might say, has kittens.

Weather. Whiskey. Death. Which of these shall we talk about, Dad, this time?

Oh, whiskey, I guess, he said. I don't drink it anymore.

He had given it up, I learned, because, he said, it no longer helped him into sleep.

But his neighbor from across the alley continued to have a drink or two as they continued to play cards, maybe two, three times a week. And something else: He is seeing the woman next door, once a week, on Sundays; they have lunch at a nearby diner, he said, then maybe they go for a ride along the canal, which cost the city more goddam money than it'll ever be worth, he said, or maybe, once in a great while, they'll go to an early movie, or what is more likely talk about going until they have talked themselves into not going, most movies today, he said, not worth watching, a conclusion he reached from many years of not having watched many movies.

And something else: He has given up left turns.

What's that? I asked. You have given up left turns? What do you mean?

What I said, he said. I no longer make left turns. They make me nervous. So I have figured out how to drive across town and back without making a single left turn.

I gave this a couple of minutes to sink in. When it did, it made sense.

Well, I said, good for you. No more left goddam turns.

When I visited him next I did not see him. He was lying in a coffin that the director of the funeral home advised us not to open. He and the neighbor woman had eaten lunch at their favorite diner, then, indulging a ride to the west side of the city to decorate a grave, a besotted driver broadsided my father's old brown Dodge, killing him probably instantly but sparing the neighbor woman, perhaps because my father had absorbed almost all of the impact.

After the funeral Johnny and I went to his house to talk about the cleaning up and the sorting out. The task would involve, perhaps, more than Emily Dickinson had in mind when she wrote

The sweeping up the heart,
And putting love away
We shall not want to use again
Until eternity.

We had, at least for the moment, pretty much swept up the heart so that what remained to be swept up was clutter that, for a small house, seemed nonetheless unmanageable. So we stood there in the dining room, scratching our heads, waiting for something beyond ourselves to reveal itself, to offer a clean solution to a very messy problem.

It occurred, behold, in the form of the card-playing neighbor from across the alley. He walked timidly and remorsefully into the dining room, saying that he knocked but nobody came to the door, asking then if he might be of help.

I looked at my brother, who was looking at me. He smiled. I nodded.

Yes, we said, perhaps in unison, you indeed can help. If you clean out Dad's house, we say, you can have everything in it.

The neighbor, incredulous, said, But what about the television?

You can have the television, we said. And everything else, including all of Dad's boxes in the basement.

He stood looking at us, first at Johnny, then at me; I believe that he was giving us a chance to change our minds. When apparently he was convinced that we were not going to budge, he said, I can start the work right away. As soon as I go get my pickup.

When he returned we told him that we wanted permission to take three items – a small ancient dresser for Johnny, an equally ancient hutch for my sister, Bernadine, and an old rocking chair for me.

I had seen the rocker when we pushed aside a faded blue wool blanket that covered the archway between the dining room and the living room. Father had used the living room as a repository for clutter that he must have considered beyond redemption. Among the many items was the rocker; and though it was lopsided and grimy and held together with binder twine and baling wire, I recognized it immediately as the rocker Grandfather had sat in as he played the accordion with the leaky bellows while singing "The Old Rugged Cross" or "Blessed Assurance" or maybe "Just a Closer Walk with Thee."

My little brother, no longer little, doubted that the chair could be brought back to life. But he was wrong. I located an old wood-worker who, after rubbing chin stubble with his right hand while rubbing one arm of the rocker with the other, declared that a resurrection might in fact be possible – if I was patient and if I might be willing to part with a substantial chunk of American currency.

I was patient. I was willing. And ultimately, behold, the old rocker was made new. Lazarus up from his grave. And its cherrywood gleamed, and there was no sign whatsoever of binder twine or baling wire. And when I sit in this rocker and rock, I can hear something, or someone, perhaps a squeak in one of the rockers or more likely an aging grandson with a voice like a German farmer, singing.

12

AT THE OUTSET of the war someone had said, poetically, Now we're in it, we have to win it.

Sitting in Urie's barber shop, I watch and listen.

Too bad Roosevelt isn't alive to enjoy this, Leland Bonham says.

Truman did the right thing, says Virgil Schmidt. Besides, he didn't have much choice. It was us or them.

I didn't need a haircut, having had my ears lowered, as they say, the Saturday before. But I wanted to browse the *Sporting News*. And I wanted to hear what some of the men had to say about the dropping of two atomic bombs. Before long the president would defend his decision to drop the bombs by saying, *I realize the tragic significance of the atomic bomb. Its production and its use were not lightly undertaken by this government. But we knew that our enemies were on the search for it. We know now how close they were to finding it. And we know the disaster which would come to this nation, and to all peaceful nations, to all civilizations, if they had found it first.*

Did you read that story in yesterday's paper about the history of dynamite? asks Leland Bonham. It was discovered by a guy named Nobel. He wanted farmers to use it to clear out tree stumps.

Ora Brant is in the chair. He is the local undertaker and the owner of a dry goods store. He mumbles something, but the words can't make their way through the lather.

President Truman had called the bomb's devastation "a black rain of ruin." He said, on the front page of the *Beacon*, "We have spent two billion dollars on the greatest scientific gamble in history – and won."

I wasn't joking about buying me a new Buick with whitewall tires, Stocker says.

I'm staying with the Plymouth, says Virgil.

I'm going to buy me a dozen cartons of Camels, Leland says, and smoke all of them beautiful little fuckers at once.

You'll have smoke coming out your ears, says Cloyd Stocker.

Not to mention his ass, adds Virgil.

Enough lather has been removed from Brant's face so that I can see him grinning. He is a devoted Baptist who loves to linger in the presence of sin.

Tree stumps, says Leland. Shitfire.

It's all over now but the shouting, Stocker says.

Tomorrow I'll turn thirteen. Last Tuesday I delivered sixty-seven papers to sixty-seven elated and bewildered customers, many of them waiting outside for me to hand them a copy of the *Beacon*. Last Saturday I watched Doc and Rusty swap quarters at the pinball machine, watched the girl behind the counter scoop ice cream into dishes and cover it with chocolate, strawberry, butterscotch, watched Johnny Moulton limp with undaunted gusto as he swept sawdust into a pile that with an oversized dustpan he delivered into a cardboard box. And last Sunday, after Sunday school and church, I listened to music and sports on my radio until my ears burned.

Enola Gay, Virgil says. That's the plane that carried the first bomb. Little Boy. That's the name of the first bomb. So why didn't the Japanese surrender after the dropping of Little Boy?

They believed we had only one bomb, says Leland. They believed they could survive that first bomb and still win the war.

Hirohito is a fartknocker, says Stocker. I'd like to see someone kick his slanteyed ass up somewhere between his shoulder blades.

I'd like to be that someone, says Leland.

Well, says Virgil, it's like Stocker said before. It's all over now but the shouting.

Urie splashes Ora's face with something whose smell reaches all the way to where I am sitting on the green bench. Ora continues to grin, as if remembering a joke he can't stop remembering.

Urie grimaces, showing his bad teeth. He says, My wife says it's all a part of God's plan.

Many months ago my grandmother called and asked me to go to the basement of the United Brethren church to look for her Bible; she believed she left it there, she said, last night following prayer meeting. And if I find it, would I mind bringing it over?

Of course I'll find it, I said. And of course I'll bring it over.

But, dammit, I couldn't find it. I had gone to the church, to the basement, expecting to see the Bible lying on one of the wooden folding chairs in the small room that served as a gathering place for Wednesday night services. But the book was not lying on one of the chairs, nor was it lying under or beside one of them. To help in the search I had turned on all of the basement lights, those in the larger room as well as those in the smaller one; I supposed that plenty of light, together with the fact that Grandmother's Bible was a large, leather-bound, dog-eared King James, would make it easy to spot the prodigal. But I could see no evidence of it anywhere.

It is logical that when you lose something you go first to where you believe you last had it in your possession. Then, not finding it there, you go to the next most likely spot. Not finding it there, you go. . . . And so on. But the amazing thing is not that you move from one spot to another but that, as you do, you come somehow to believe that, yes, probably this *is* where you left, and thus lost, it, regardless of how utterly unlikely that place might be. I went from the small room to the larger one, then back to the small room, then to the kitchen in the northwest corner, where I looked on the table and the tops of the chairs and the top of the stove and inside the refrigerator and in the oven and in the cupboards and everywhere else before returning to the small room where for the third time I looked where already I had looked two times before, including the top of the pulpit.

The basement of the United Brethren church was essentially a rectangular concrete vault divided, as already noted, into a large room, a small room, and a kitchen. Wooden folding chairs, many of them, lay stacked in the northeast corner of the large room, a room commodious enough, in fact, to accommodate wedding receptions (my own eventually included) and after-burial dinners and suppers.

No finishing work was evident in any of the rooms. The floors, concrete. The walls, concrete. The ceilings, unfinished pine.

I roamed those rooms that early evening for forty days and forty nights, it seemed, looking where I had looked before, inhaling the rich aromas of pine and dampened concrete. That morning a drizzle had fallen and the concrete had taken it in, and now as I searched for Grandmother's elusive Bible the concrete released it, slowly, and with deep inhalations I took it in. Believe this much: There are few sensory highs capable of competing with that offered by damp, cool concrete joined to pine; only a backyard cave, dug by two young boys whose mother stood in the kitchen wringing her hands, could reasonably compete. And, too, there is the matter of what the air in the basement might have retained, the gauzy effluvium of breath that once upon a time were words, hanging around. Is it possible that I inhaled not only dampness and coolness and pine but also portions of Paul's letter to Philemon? *Yea, brother, let me have joy of thee in the Lord: refresh my bowels in the Lord.*

And it occurs to me that it is almost time for supper. Reluctantly I switch off the lights; I will have to tell Grandmother that I failed to find her Bible. Perhaps the minister spotted it and took it home or to his study. Did she think to call him?

No, she didn't, because she found the Bible herself. It was in her bedroom, on the stand beside the bed, just where she had left it. But she did make a phone call – to my mother, to tell her that I would not be home for supper; I would be eating that meal with my grandmother. Milk toast and homemade chocolate pie.

I called the nurse an unkind name because she betrayed me. She had told me that, yes, I could have some warm milk toast following the surgery and that it would taste ever so delicious. I was four. I believed her at the time she said it and even until the moment that the physician, Dr. Galloway, sent me to sleep with his white cloth dampened with ether. I had requested the milk toast because I considered it a delicacy: toast cut into small squares stirred into a bowl of warm milk. I would endure the removal of my tonsils if at the completion of their removal I might have a bowl of warm milk toast.

But the nurse in her white dress and her wide white smile betrayed me. After I had returned from Eden and she had brought me the bowl of milk toast and had helped me with my first sip (I could see no squares of toast floating in the milk), I felt a burning in my throat like the hell I said I hoped she'd fry forever in – or words to that effect. And I called her an unkind name, screamed it and choked it out, a name that I had heard my father use, no doubt, one unkind enough to cause my mother's face to go uncommonly blank, then uncommonly red, as if embarrassed, then uncommonly blue, as if angry – but not at her son as much as at the nurse, who had fed me milk too warm for my tender swallowing mechanism to accept without some form of rebellion. Thus the burning in my throat that in turn prompted the vociferation that somehow shaped the unkind word that my mother dozens of times over the ensuing centuries, telling the story, refused to repeat. To this day I know it only as *an unkind name.*

I was happy that evening sharing supper with Grandmother Anna Steierl Yock, old German woman from the wilds of Karlshuld, because in spite of the trauma I experienced at the hands of the turncoat nurse I continued to adore milk toast; and I would be a fool, and dishonest, if I didn't say that Anna's chocolate pie was the tastiest ever to have graced a pie pan. So there we were, Grandmother and I, wolfing milk toast and chocolate pie, Grandmother having returned grace, a part of which she devoted to thanking her Creator for having led her to the stand beside her bed where, behold, lay her lost Bible. And might it be permissible, do you suppose, to have a second wedge?

Hindsight. It tells me what probably I should have guessed that evening had I used the brains I might have been born with – that my German grandmother knew all along where the Bible was. Her sending me to the United Brethren church had been an elaborate Krauthead ruse to lead me into a temptation I didn't mind at all yielding to. The milk toast was delicious, the chocolate pie divine.

The ruse had worked. Jesus. Is it any wonder, then, that the Allied forces had such a horrendous time during those inexorable months preceding Hiroshima and Nagasaki freeing Paris? Overtaking Berlin?

Ora steps down from the chair to permit Stocker his turn. Stocker is almost as wide as he is tall. He crawls into the chair as if scaling a mountain. Urie covers him with a white sheet, lowers the back of the chair until Stocker lies like a snow-covered mound, his face a sturdy, self-satisfied headstone.

Each day during the past week I delivered papers that told more than a boy could understand. How high exactly is thirty-nine thousand feet, the altitude from which the first bomb, Little Boy, was dropped? I could imagine the height at which the bomb detonated, six hundred sixty yards; that would be the distance of six football fields plus six first-and-tens.

But how brief exactly is one ten-thousandth of a second, that unimaginable twinkling of an eye during which a heat of three hundred thousand degrees centigrade was generated? The *Beacon* gave me these numbers, but I could not fathom them, not even when advised that the heat flattened and disintegrated and melted everything – brick and wood and fabric and flesh – within a two thousand-yard radius of the hypocenter. *Hy-po-cen-ter*. Hotter there than – where? Sister Hook's inferno? The place I would gladly have consigned the nurse to? The middle of my family's ill-fated kitchen?

Tomorrow I will turn thirteen. After delivering the early morning papers I'll go, of course, to Sunday school, then remain to listen to what I am guessing will be the preacher's text – a time to plant, a time to reap; a time to rise up, a time to lie down. Or maybe this: Time and chance happen to us all.

But at the moment I am sitting on the green bench in Urie's barber shop, watching Urie, listening to the faithful review the past as they anticipate the future, one of them certain that the Cubs and the Tigers will meet in the Series, another singing the praises of welterweight Rocky Graziano, another worshiping at the feet of

Cadet footballers Glenn Davis and Doc Blanchard. Through it all Stocker lies silent as a log. Urie tends the sturdy, self-satisfied face with a razor whose edge had been honed against a band of leather, *strop* both its name and its sound, and hearing that sound I think of my buddy R. D., of his taking a BB almost in the eye, of his describing the whipping he took from his father, *strop strop strop* against the boy's flesh, of R. D. grinning as he showed me the marvelous BB – and of R. D. moving recently with his mother and father to a big city to experience whatever the big city holds in store.

Urie without saying anything excuses himself to visit the back room. Stocker remains inert. I turn the pages of the *Sporting News* without looking down at the pages. It is another Saturday in my small hometown, a warm Saturday in August, and the amazing thing is that the town looks pretty much the same as it had before Little Boy and Fat Man were dropped. But there seems to be something not quite definable waiting, or maybe lurking, beneath the surface. Tomorrow I will turn thirteen. Mother said that when I was born Dr. Galloway said, He's big for his size. And big I was – almost eleven pounds. The amazing thing is that things keep going on. After delivering the papers I'll make the other rounds – pool hall, drugstore, grocery store, and so on. Tomorrow, after Sunday school and church, I'll probably walk my grandmother home, then, at her insistence, stay for a piece of the birthday cake I know she'll surprise me with. Already I can see myself at the kitchen table. Between us sits the cake, large enough to feed a mid-sized army. Watch now as Grandmother hands me a box of Diamond matches. I remove one to strike it against the side of the box. Watch as I light each of the thirteen candles and then, having closed my eyes to make a wish, with a mighty exhalation blow them out.